The Parables
Of Jesus

Applications For Contemporary Life

Cycle B

Richard Gribble, CSC

CSS Publishing Company, Inc., Lima, Ohio

THE PARABLES OF JESUS, CYCLE B

Copyright © 1999 by
CSS Publishing Company, Inc.
Lima, Ohio

Scripture quotations are from the *New Revised Standard Version of the Bible*, copyright 1989 by the Division of Christian Education of the National Council of the Churches of Christ in the USA. Used by permission.

Library of Congress Cataloging-in-Publication Data

Gribble, Richard.
    The parables of Jesus : applications for contemporary life, Cycle A / Richard Gribble.
        p.   cm.
    Includes bibliographical references
    ISBN 0-7880-1197-9 (pbk.)
    1. Jesus Christ—Parables—Sermons. 2. Sermons, American. I. Title.
BT375.2.G73   1998
251'.6—DC20   98-5191
                                                                            CIP

This book is available in the following formats, listed by ISBN:
    0-7880-1355-6   Book
    0-7880-1356-4   Disk
    0-7880-1357-2   Sermon Prep

PRINTED IN U.S.A.

Dedication

Faith is like the tiny mustard seed that grows and becomes the greatest of all plants. The seeds of faith are present in many sources, but I have found the dedication and love of friends to be a great seedbed of faith for me. This book is dedicated to my friends in Stoughton, Massachusetts, whose seeds of faith have blossomed into a tree of goodness and life.

Preface

For almost two thousand years the Christian community throughout the world has assembled each Sunday to praise God. Gathered on the Lord's Day, the day of Christ's triumphal resurrection, Christians celebrate in word and sacrament the presence of God in our world, both our individual lives and human society collectively. While celebration of the Eucharist is a common practice for all Christian denominations, the word of God transmitted to us in Sacred Scripture is universally held to be central to worship. The Bible challenges and inspires us; it reveals the message of God and provides a road map for the faithful to follow as we daily travel the path that leads to God and eternal life.

While each individual finds a special pearl in the vast treasure of Scripture, most people agree that the Gospels present the heart of Jesus' message. Written by people of faith at different times and for varied audiences, the Gospels provide accounts of the words and deeds of Jesus Christ from his birth, through his public ministry in Israel, and culminating in his passion, death, and resurrection. The evangelists' accounts vary, but the core of Christ's teaching — faith, love of God and neighbor, forgiveness and reconciliation, and service — echoes through all four Gospels. These books of the Bible are familiar to all Christians, who are schooled in them from childhood. Each Sunday service or Mass contains a reading from one of the Gospels.

The best known literary form presented in the Gospels is the parable. Many of the parables have become Bible favorites because of their familiar, appealing, and challenging teachings. The parables of the prodigal son (Luke 15:1-32), the sower (Matthew 13:1-9, 18-23), the uncaring judge (Luke 18:1-8), the Good Shepherd (John 10:11-18), and the Good Samaritan (Luke 10:25-37) are known and quoted by Christians throughout the world.

Jesus used parables to enter into dialogue with his disciples and opponents alike. By their nature parables present their message in an indirect manner; their meaning is not obvious, but open to interpretation. Reading the parables with the eyes of a Christian approaching the third millennium, we will most probably obtain a different understanding than the first hearers of Jesus' words.

In order for the parable to maintain the timelessness of Scripture, the message contained in the story must be applied to our contemporary environment and culture. It is the awesome task of the preacher to make the Scriptures come alive for the faithful who worship in our churches. This book is my effort to apply the Gospel message to today's world with all its beauty, difficulties, and challenges.

Preachers and those wishing to understand the parables better can use this volume to open new doors of insight into the infinite treasure of Christ's message to the world. This book presents a theme and spiritual food for our daily journey, applying the parable's message in a contemporary context. Sample homily openings together with questions for reflection and challenge provide preachers with one possible road map in preparing a sermon. Lastly, each parable is analyzed through exegesis and is placed in context within the liturgical year, with the other Gospels, and the two additional Scripture lessons of the day.

This book is a combination of personal reflection, prayer, and research. As many scholars have discovered various meanings in the parables, so preachers will differ in their method of applying these powerful stories to today's world. It is my hope that the reader will find my reflections and ideas a challenge. If preachers are not challenged, if they cannot convince themselves of the importance and contemporary viability of the message of Scripture, they will never convince those who hear God's word and seek guidance in its application. The messages of the parables outlined in this book speak to me of the need for God. May those who use this volume experience that same need.

Richard Gribble, CSC

Table Of Contents

Introduction

Gospel, Parable, And The Traditions
Of Mark And John

The parables of Jesus are possibly the best known sections of Sacred Scripture. Reading the Gospels it is impossible to proceed far without encountering one of the many accounts that have been classified by scholars and novices alike as parables. Christians have been schooled from childhood on the important messages and teachings of the four Gospel evangelists that have been transmitted as stories told by Jesus to his disciples and opponents. In order to understand more completely the message and significance of Jesus' words, it is important to gain some insight into the literary form of gospel, where parables were used, and what precisely is meant by the concept of parable. The fact that the Synoptic authors and John use parables in different ways also necessitates an understanding of the tradition of the evangelists, their sources, audience, and purpose of composition. This chapter serves to introduce the reader to the concepts of gospel and parable and how they are utilized in the work of Saints Mark and John.

The Gospel Tradition

The word "gospel" finds its roots in the Greek *euangelion,* meaning the good news. For the people of the early Church *euangelion* signified not a book that chronicled and emphasized the significance of Jesus' words and actions, but rather, the good news of Messianic salvation present in Christ's life. Such good tidings were first proclaimed by the prophet Isaiah (52:7): "How beautiful upon the mountains are the feet of the messenger who announces peace, who brings good news, who announces salvation, who says to Zion, 'Your God reigns.' " Jesus preached the good news (Mark 1:15, Matthew 11:5, and Luke 4:18) to all who would listen. The good news was also found in the apostolic preaching concerning Christ and the salvation that is found in him (Acts 5:42 and Romans 1:1ff).

The Gospels and the epistles of the New Testament were the first written sources that described Jesus and his message of salvation. The Gospels record Christ's words and deeds as they were remembered by others; they were not written by Jesus. The writings of the evangelists may be precisely what Jesus said and did, but it is much more likely that the accuracy we assume in contemporary historical writing is not present here. This should not be disturbing for several reasons. First, since there are four different Gospel accounts of Jesus' activities, written at different times for various reasons, it would be virtually impossible for total agreement in dates, times, and specific actions. This is clearly evident when one compares the Synoptic accounts with each other and especially with John. The Gospels were not all (possibly none) written by eyewitnesses to the events related; the authors, therefore, used sources to generate their works. Oral tradition and written sources were combined with the opinion and agenda of the writer to produce accounts which portray the purpose and message of Jesus in a particular light.

The Gospels are not biographies of Jesus nor are they accurate historical documents. The evangelists did not try to relate everything that Jesus did (John 21:25). Rather, they selected material from sources available to fashion a written account of Christ's life that would be understandable to readers, transmit the message of salvation, and portray Jesus as he was perceived by the writer. The Gospels were not written to be accurate histories; they are writings of faith. One need look no further than the difference between the Synoptics and John on the length of Jesus' public ministry (one year versus three) to realize the lack of historicity in the texts. The objective of the evangelists in general was to demonstrate the ministry of the Messiah from its favorable beginning in Galilee, to its tragic conclusion in Jerusalem, and its ultimate triumph through resurrection. Modern historic writing demands a detailed and accurate chronology, but the lack of historical accuracy in the Gospels does not compromise the writer's purpose nor deflate the importance of Christ's ministry.

The Gospels were written many years after the events they describe using sources available to the evangelists. Mark, judged today by scholars as the first Gospel written, used literary works, including the Roman catechesis of Peter, and oral tradition as its principle sources. Matthew and Luke used Mark, supplementing it with a common "Q" (German *Quelle)* source and material particular to each writer. John, standing apart from the synoptic tradition, produced a very different account. Some scholars suggest he wrote to supplement the Synoptics and others believe that he wrote a completely different account with no knowledge of the accounts of Matthew, Mark, and Luke. Close similarities in all accounts of the crucifixion, however, indicate that this was a well-known event in the apostolic age and that it had been communicated in a consistent manner in oral and written sources.

The Synoptic Gospels all follow a basic format. The first part of each account describes Jesus' preparation for his public ministry and his baptism by John. Next, the evangelists describe in various forms of detail the ministry of Jesus in Galilee. The Messiah's journey with his disciples from Galilee to Jerusalem, complete with predictions of Jesus' death, are then related. All three evangelists conclude their accounts in Jerusalem with a chronicle of the passion, death, and resurrection of the Lord. The aforementioned similarity of the passion narratives tells scholars that this section of these Gospels was probably written first.

Those familiar with Sacred Scripture are well aware that there are many other writings of the period that are not part of the canon. This fact raises the question of how the canon was produced and what criteria were used in its selection. Four basic criteria determined the canonical status of the many sacred writings. Apostolic origin was the first criterion. Authorship by one of the chosen twelve or those known as apostles in the early church gave immediate credibility to any writing. Next, those charged with developing the canon looked at the community addressed in writings. This criterion was especially applicable in the Pauline corpus and other writings ascribed to Paul. Conformity to the rule of faith was a third criterion. A document may have been attributed to an apostle, but if its content was inconsistent with the message of salvation as understood by the people of the day, then its validity was highly suspect and its importance suppressed. Lastly, as a review of the volumes of apocrypha and pseudepigrapha reveals, there are numerous writings that seem to fit the basic criteria set for acceptability, yet they are not part of the canon of Scripture. Thus, the element of chance in the final selection must not be discounted.

Parable In Concept And Use

In order to describe the purpose and meaning of Jesus' words which we know as parable, some basic understanding of this term must be given. One definition suitable for our purposes is: "Every parable is a story; this story conveys a lesson so that the parable has a double meaning, the story and the lesson; the parable's purpose is to effect a change in the hearer, to lead to decision or action; and the lesson always is religious or moral."[1] In modern usage the term parable should be and usually is reserved for those stories which are drawn from ordinary everyday life, which have a religious or moral lesson conveyed indirectly, and which are intended to convince or persuade and to bring the hearer to decision or action.

Each parable has four distinct characteristics. First, parables are narratives which tell stories, generally of a popular or folk nature. These stories are told, however, on two levels, the literal and the topical. Secondly, parabolic stories convey a message that is indirect, often only implicit. Next, parables are far more than entertainment; they are told to bring about a change of mind or even better a change of heart (the Greek *metanoia*) in the hearer. The call to conversion is also heard in these message-laden stories. Hearers of the parable cannot be neutral; they must accept or reject the lesson. In this sense parables are rhetorical. Lastly, parables, in conveying a religious or ethical message, also present a challenge in living the interrelationship between the human and the divine.

Literary criticism demonstrates the similarities and differences between parable and allegory. In a parable one single point of comparison is presented; the details of the story have no independent significance. This second idea distinguishes parable from allegory, for in the latter each detail has a symbolic significance. This distinction should not be presented too rigorously, however, for it is not uncommon, especially in an extended parable, that certain details are inserted precisely because they suit the intended application. A rigid distinction is also unwise when one sees that the concept of parable in Scripture is broad, like the Hebrew concept of *mashal*, a term that includes figurative speech of every kind.

Three basic forms of parable are found in the Gospels. Similitude, the most concise form, tells a typical or recurrent event from real life that would be familiar to all hearers. The similitude gains its persuasiveness by recounting what is widely recognized as true. Examples of this form include the parables of the lost coin (Luke 15:8-10) and the growing seed (Mark 4:26-29). The form labeled "parable" is often (though not always) longer and more detailed than the similitude. This literary genre tells a story, not about something recurrent in real life, but about a one-time event which is fictitious. Although they are fables, parables never indulge the fanciful or fantastic; they remain true to life. Usually narrated in the past tense, parables derive their cogency from the single, vivid, and fresh way they engage the hearer. Numerous Synoptic parables use this form including the stories of the persistent widow (Luke 18:1-8), and the two sons (Matthew 21:28-30). Exemplary story is the third form of Gospel parable. Like the other two forms, exemplary story presents an implied comparison between an event drawn from real life and the reality of the moral or religious order. Rather than drawing a distinction between two very different things (as do similitude and parable), the exemplary story presents a single example, one specific case, which illustrates a general principle. Luke's Gospel contains all four exemplary stories — the Good Samaritan (10:29-37), the rich fool (12:16-21), the rich man and Lazarus (16:19-31), and the Pharisee and tax collector (18:9-14).

The timelessness of the Gospel message is present in the way parables serve their twofold purpose to present a story with a lesson.

Parables derive their material from real life, from the everyday world of family and friends, work and worship. They are always drawn from the experiences of Jesus and his audience. For the most part the parables are set in the rural life of Israel. Though the setting is contemporary and common, the experiences that are narrated transcend that time and place; they speak to hearers of all ages and cultures. Although the material is drawn from everyday life, some parables have elements which move from the ordinary to the extraordinary, such as the yeast as leaven (Matthew 13:33 and Luke 13:20-21) or the unforgiving servant (Matthew 18:23-35). These features demonstrate that parables deal with matters transcending ordinary life.

The concept of parable, although most common to us in the Gospels, has deep roots in the Mediterranean world, where it was used as a teaching technique. In Greece and Rome parables were employed by rhetoricians, politicians, and philosophers, including Socrates and Aristotle. In Israel parables were used by the Old Testament prophets as well as Jewish rabbis who were contemporaries of Jesus. In the Gospels a parable may be a proverb, such as "Doctor, cure yourself" (Luke 4:23), as well as its more common use as story and lesson.

Any discussion of the parables must ask what was Jesus' purpose in using this indirect method to proclaim his message? Scholars today generally agree that Christ did not use parables primarily to convey general religion and ethical truths or as weapons of warfare for defense or attack. Thus, Jesus did not use parables to convey information or enter into debate. Rather, he used them to win his audience to his view; they became instruments of dialogue between Jesus and his disciples. The Lord's aim was to engage his hearers' attention and to gain their assent in order that they could adopt his views. Indeed, Jesus used parables as a means of dialogue where he presented his views and perceptions and anticipated the objections of his listeners. The parable became the primary vehicle whereby Jesus taught both his disciples and his opponents.

Why did Jesus teach some of his most important lessons using parables? Mark 4:10-12 suggests that he wanted to conceal his teachings from those outside the immediate fold: "When he was alone, those who were around him along with the twelve asked him about the parables. And he said to them, 'To you has been given the secret of the kingdom of God, but for those outside, everything comes in parables; in order that "they may indeed look, but not perceive, and may indeed listen, but not understand; so that they may not turn again and be forgiven." ' " Scholars have wrestled with these verses, perceiving them to be contradictory to Jesus' need to teach all people. However, it is probable that Christ used parables to conceal his teaching and make it more difficult for those who sought to find fault and accuse him of sedition. Additional reasons to use parables were to reveal his message to his disciples and as a tool to disarm his listeners. At times Jesus sought to penetrate the hostility and hardness of heart of his listeners by means of a parable.

The Tradition Of John

The Gospel of John presents the life, teachings, and message of Jesus in ways unique to the whole of the New Testament. Any serious reader of the Scriptures is familiar with the Synoptic tradition of Matthew, Mark, and Luke — its common sources, consistent chronology of Jesus' life, and literary format, including the frequent use of parables. John's Gospel, written later and for a different audience, presents a distinctive view of Christ, consistent in teaching and understanding with the Synoptics, but with a unique chronology, approach, and style compared with the other three Gospel evangelists.

Authorship of the fourth Gospel has been debated by scholars over the centuries. Ireneaus, Bishop of Lyons, (180 A.D.) was the first to ascribe the account to John the Apostle, a belief that was common in the late second century.[2] Corroboration of apostolic authorship is provided in the text of the Gospel. It is clear that the author is a Jew familiar with Palestine and an eyewitness to the events related. The precision with which the author identifies places, such as the Pool of Bethsaida (5:2), indicates exact knowledge of the region. The nomenclature of the Gospel also reflects the Judean scene before 70 A.D., the date of the Roman destruction of the Temple and the Diaspora.

Confusion on authorship comes about when scholars compare the fourth Gospel with other books ascribed to John — his three letters and the Book of Revelation. The Gospel and epistles were physically written by one well-schooled in Greek while Revelation was penned in a very rough, even crude, form of Greek common to the Semitic tradition of a Galilean fisherman. Additionally, the language and literary tradition of Revelation is much different than the other books ascribed to John the Apostle. In order to explain this disparity, Scripture exegetes have concluded that the Gospel and Epistles of John were actually written by someone employed by the Apostle as a disciple-scribe whose knowledge of Greek was vastly superior to his own. This does not contradict Johannine authorship, especially when one considers it was quite common in the period for scribes to write in the names of others.

Physical authorship by someone other than John the Apostle is also indicated by textual inconsistencies and additions to the original manuscript. At times in this Gospel the discourses of Jesus are interrupted for no apparent reason. Chapter 14 concludes with Jesus exhorting his disciples to "Rise, let us be on our way," indicating a shift in location and the end of a teaching. Yet, Chapter 15 begins with another teaching, "I am the vine," that appears to have been added by a later interpolator. Additions to the original text are seen best in the whole of Chapter 21. The Gospel clearly ends with the evangelist's teaching that Jesus did many other things not recorded, yet the book continues with its famous post-Resurrection narrative. Scholars today generally agree that the Gospel of John was dictated over a long period of time, with its completion and final ordering done after the apostle's death.

Debate over the date and place of composition of John's Gospel has also evolved over time. In the late nineteenth century scholars believed the book to have been composed in the late second century from evidence of influences not present in the apostolic age. This belief was bound up with the idea that the Gospel was of little historical value and could not have been the work of an eyewitness. As we have seen above, however, contemporary scholarship has demonstrated the consistency of this Gospel with the Jewish tradition of John the Baptist and Jesus. The Gospel's use of the writings of Ignatius of Antioch, Justin Martyr, and several references in the Gnostic gospels make it difficult to suggest any date later than the end of the first century for the Gospel's composition. The strongest and most ancient tradition has placed the Gospel's composition at Ephesus.

The Gospel of John, although understood as a separate evangelical effort that relates Jesus' life and message, still maintains important connections to the Synoptic writers. The Synoptic tradition in several ways is assumed by John in his message. He takes it for granted, as one example, that the reader knows the apostles, for the Fourth Gospel provides no introduction. More importantly, John omits basic data on the life of Christ, including his birth and infancy, and the institution of the Eucharist in his narrative. The author assumes these items, preferring to concentrate in his prologue on the major theological themes of the book and in chapter 6 on an exposition of Eucharistic theology. Many passages in this Gospel would be unclear without the Synoptic tradition as background. The evangelist's purpose is not to supplement or correct the accounts of Matthew, Mark, and Luke, but rather to give his own testimony without regard to style, chronology, or method of his predecessors.

While a detailed explanation of the characteristics of John's Gospel is beyond the purpose of this overview, it is important to understand how certain ideas of this Gospel are associated with the literary genre of parable. Scholars disagree on whether John uses parables in the same manner as the Synoptics. Exegetes point out that John uses many of the same metaphors and symbols of the other evangelists, but their format is more allegory than parable. Nevertheless, the symbolism, present in the pericope of the gate and the shepherd (John 10:1-10), is quite complex and serves to profess an important message, as do all parables. John's use of symbol is his basic pattern of relating the teachings of Jesus to a wider audience in time and space. The evangelist's use of the symbols of light and dark to represent life and death, Christ against sin, is portrayed throughout the Gospel. Universal symbology is present in such characters as Lazarus and the beloved disciple representing all Christians, not merely their historical personages. Mary, the Mother of God, is symbolic for the universal church. The message of the parable in the Synoptics is thus presented through use of symbols in the Gospel of John.

The Tradition Of Mark

The Gospel of Mark, the shortest of the four Gospels, is nonetheless fundamental to the whole of the New Testament. Scholars today are certain that it was the first Gospel to be composed and that it served as the basic source for Matthew and Luke. Mark does not present the material of the "Q" source and thus is shorter than the other Synoptics, but the events related are generally described more vividly and with greater detail than the same incidents' depiction in Matthew and Luke. Parables and the teachings of Jesus are not scattered through the text but rather are grouped by the evangelist in readily identifiable sections of the Gospel. Mark's Gospel gives the reader a unique vision of Jesus, his ministry, and the significance of his life.

The tradition which attributes this Gospel to Mark has little reason to be challenged. Neither Scripture nor history speaks of anyone named Mark to be particularly prominent in the early Church or close to Jesus. Scholars conclude that there would have been no good reason to attribute the work to Mark unless a man by that name had been known to be the author. Irenaeus and Origen both ascribe authorship of this Gospel to Mark. The major question that is unresolved by scholars is the identity of Mark. Many scholars over the centuries have stated that John Mark, mentioned in the Acts of the Apostles 12:12, 25, is the author, but this is not certain. The language used in the Gospel does give us some insight into the origins of the author. The text is written in rough Greek and contains several words never translated from Aramaic. This has led some commentators to believe that the text is a translation from Aramaic or that the author was not lettered in Greek. Others believe that the language demonstrates that the author was a Palestinian whose mother tongue was Aramaic.

Similarities between Mark and Matthew led scholars in earlier centuries to conclude that Mark was an abbreviated version of Matthew, but today scholars are convinced that Mark was the prototype for all the Synoptics. The Gospel's date of composition has been established based on other known dates. Papias and Irenaeus both concluded that Mark's Gospel was written after Saint Peter died in the persecution of Nero in 64 A.D. Scholars today additionally conclude that Matthew and Luke, written by contemporaries of Jesus, were definitely composed before the end of the first century. Since Mark is the primary source for the other Synoptics, exegetes have concluded that this Gospel was most probably written between 64 and 75 A.D. This would have allowed the Gospel to circulate, become known, and thus be accepted as a primary source for other evangelists.

The tradition has placed the composition of Mark's Gospel in Rome. Irenaeus, Clement of Alexandria (as quoted by Eusebius), and the anti-Marcionate Prologue all attest to Rome as the Gospel's place of origin. Scholars today provide evidence that verifies this hypothesis. Mark's explanation of Aramaic terms such as *Boanerges* and *talitha cum* suggests an audience unfamiliar with the language and customs of Palestine. Moreover, Mark uses Latin terms, such as denarius, legion, and centurion, more than any other evangelist, giving additional evidence that the audience targeted was Roman. Lastly, the text of the Gospel indicates that its readers were members of a community that had known or was expecting persecution for the faith. All of these ideas are consistent with Roman origin. Although in recent years Antioch and even Palestine have been offered as alternatives, the preponderance of opinion places the Gospel's origin with Gentile Christians in Rome.

Early Christian belief in the imminence of the Parousia led to a desire to preserve the memory of Jesus. Leaders in the community needed a vehicle to persuade non-believers of Jesus' supernatural nature and to help converts to discover the implication of their newfound discipleship. The composition of Mark's Gospel was a major accomplishment toward achievement of this goal. Circumstances of the environment in which Jesus was to be remembered exercised a strong influence on the nature of what information and memories about the Messiah were preserved. In viewing Jesus' life Mark was not interested in convincing his audience of the sinlessness of Jesus and the truthfulness of his claims and teaching; these were assumed and thus were not part of his text. Mark is interested rather in demonstrating the Messiahship of Christ and outlining the difficult road that must be traversed by any and all who wish to follow his lead.

Different opinions have been presented as to the sources used by Mark to present his case. Some have suggested that the evangelist used a Greek translation of Matthew, known as the Palestinian Catechesis of Peter. This view, however, is inconsistent with the belief that Mark's Gospel was the first written. It is more likely that Mark used the Roman Catechesis of Peter, who wrote down as accurately as he could remember the things said and done by Jesus. While the exact source of Mark's Gospel cannot be definitively known, it is clear to scholars that much of Mark's material was already grouped in units that the evangelist merely reproduced in his text. For example, in Mark 2:1—3:6 a series of five conflicts between Christ and the Pharisees in Galilee is presented: on forgiveness of sins (2:1-12), eating with publicans and sinners (2:13-17), fasting (2:18-22), plucking of ears of corn on the Sabbath (2:23-28), and healing on the Sabbath (3:1-6). Later a series of six conflicts that appear to be one unit is reproduced: mission of Jesus and baptism of John (11:27-33), parable of the wicked husbandman (12:1-12), tribute to Caesar (12:13-17), resurrection (12:18-27), greatest commandment (12:28-34), and origin of the Messiah (12:35-37). These grouped sections of narrative were, in the opinion of many scholars, extracted by Mark from a source and inserted directly into his Gospel.

Mark's Gospel intentionally was not written as a historical narrative, but it does divide nicely into two major sections. Mark 1:1—8:26 places emphasis on Jesus and his teaching that is directed to the crowds. The message, presented most vividly in the parables of chapter 4, is concerned with the coming of God's kingdom. After 8:31 a major change in the direction of the text is noticeable. The miraculous healings so prevalent in the first half of the Gospel are now rare and the emphasis shifts more to Jesus' teaching, now directed to the apostles, that assumes knowledge of Jesus' Messiahship. God's will is that the Messiah's word should be carried out with the knowledge that suffering will occur for both Jesus and his followers. These two sections are connected by Peter's confession of faith (8:27-30), the first time Jesus is recognized as Messiah by a human.

Mark's Gospel highlights certain major themes. The central message of the Gospel is the manifestation of the suffering Son of God. Like Matthew he sees Jesus as Messiah, but he concentrates more on the sufferings of Christ. This emphasis leads the evangelist to three related ideas: (1) Jesus asks his followers to suffer as he did. (2) Jesus warned his followers that suffering would be their lot. (3) The Lord promised great and sure rewards to those who endured suffering without losing their faith. Another theme particular to Mark is his concept of the Messianic secret. If Jesus was the Messiah why did he not claim it; why was he not recognized? Mark responds by saying that Jesus deliberately sought to keep his Messiahship a secret. Some commentators suggest that the false notion of Messiahship held by so many Jews in Jesus' day forced him to keep his role as savior and redeemer under wraps. Others suggest that it was a literary device used by the evangelist to help accent the climax at 8:27-30 in Peter's confession, "You are the Messiah."

---

1. Madeleine I. Boucher, *The Parables* Revised Edition (Wilmington, Delaware: Michael Glazier, Inc., 1983), p. 19.

2. Ireneaus also identified the author as "the one whom Jesus loved" (John 13:23). There is no other figure in the Gospel that corresponds to the beloved disciple. This understanding of John as the beloved disciple is commonly held today.

Advent 1

Chapter 1

Watching For The
Coming Of The Lord

Mark 13:32-37

---

*"But about that day or hour no one knows, neither the
angels in heaven, nor the Son, but only the Father.
Beware, keep alert; for you do not know when the time
will come. It is like a man going on a journey, when he
leaves home and puts his slaves in charge, each with
his work, and commands the doorkeeper to be on the
watch. Therefore, keep awake — for you do not know
when the master of the house will come, in the evening,
or at midnight, or at cockcrow, or at dawn, or else he
may find you asleep when he comes suddenly. And what
I say to you I say to all: Keep awake."*

Theme

The ideas of watchfulness, preparation, and readiness are clearly
present in this passage from Jesus' eschatological discourse. We
wait for many things in our lives, some of which are so routine that
we give them no second thought, and others which require much
preparation. We can generally plan for future events which have a
fixed arrival date, but there are certain things that require daily
vigilance because we know not the day or the hour of their coming
into our lives. Jesus' parable of the doorkeeper challenges us to be
always watchful as we await the coming of the Lord.

Spiritual Food For The Journey

It seems that life is one period of preparation after another. When we are in school we work hard in the primary grades so as to advance to the intermediate level. Then we must prepare again for high school and so again for college. Even when we get to the college or university we prepare ourselves for the first job. We labor long and hard hours to prepare for our next assignment or the promotion that is our goal. We prepare ourselves at school, in our job, in fact, in every facet of life. One might logically ask, will I ever be ready?

The simple answer, of course, is no. Life requires that we move from situation to situation, relationship to relationship, job to job. The first time when we think we are fully ready and become complacent, life throws us a curveball and we find ourselves lost. There is a need to be always watchful and make preparations because we don't know what life will bring our way.

Watchfulness in our relationship with the Lord is of the greatest importance. If we slack off and fail to prepare ourselves in a relationship or job we may lose a friend or position. But if we fail to be alert, make preparations, and watch for the Lord, then we may miss God and lose salvation in the process. Let us always be watchful for God's coming. We will never know the day or the hour.

Application Of The Parable To Contemporary Life

Sermon Openings
1. Imagine picking up the Sunday paper, opening it, and reading in giant letters, **Jesus Christ Will Return on December 25!** What would we do? How would we react to this astonishing information? I think there would be two basic reactions. Some of us, out of fear, would change our lives immediately. The Lord is coming and we are not ready! We might start going to church more often, probably every day. Prayer would become a much higher priority in life. We would pray not only in the morning and evening, but

many times each day. We would seek reconciliation, with a member of our family, neighbor, co-worker, and certainly with God. Others might have a very different response. Some of us might do nothing differently. Some in a defeatist attitude might say, "There is nothing I can do at this late hour. God has already decided my fate. I might as well continue what I have been doing all along." There are others who might not change a thing that they are doing, but not in a defeatist mode. Some of us hopefully would say, "Isn't this the event for which the world has been waiting? Isn't this the reason for which I came into the world?" Possession of such an attitude would allow us to continue doing what we have always been doing, confident that our preparations have been sound.

Life, it seems, is one big process of preparation. When we are young each year seems to be preparation for the next. When we are in elementary school we prepare for junior high, and in junior high we work hard to ready ourselves for high school. The preparation process continues into college and to our first job, but it does not end there. One job leads to a second or to the promotion which we justly deserve. One might naturally say, "Will we ever be fully ready?"

On this First Sunday of Advent we celebrate our need to prepare. In this season we prepare for the Lord's coming in history, but we also prepare for his Second Coming at the end of time (the Parousia). Today our readings focus on this latter idea. Jesus' birth into history happened one time; it will never occur again. We can celebrate this Advent and prepare, however, because the Lord can and will return into our hearts if the invitation which he extends is accepted. Jesus will come, however, as the Gospel indicates, when we least expect. Therefore, we must be ready. Advent is a time for us to reevaluate our lives and see how we have been doing with the invitations extended by God.

2. As individuals and community we are constantly waiting. We wait in lines in the market, the bank, and stores. We wait for events. We wait for the big game to start on television, for the movie to begin in the theater, for the arrival of a family member or friend at the airport. Most of the time we wait with certain knowledge that

something will happen at a prescribed time. We all wait for birthdays (even though at times we may want to forget), but we know precisely when the date will arrive. We wait for the next three-day weekend, but again we know the event's exact time. We wait for Christmas, but have learned from childhood that Jesus arrives on December 25.

Sometimes we wait for things that eventually will come, but there is no way to know when they will happen. Farmers wait patiently for the rain to nurture the fields, but there is no way to predict its arrival precisely. After a long winter all of us look forward to the blossoms, flowers, and budding trees as signs of spring, but again we cannot know when the miracle of new life will be manifest. We look forward with longing for visits from family and friends, but often do not know when they will arrive. These unexpected periods of waiting force us to prepare in a different manner. We must be more attentive and vigilant. We cannot be lazy; the event for which we wait may happen and we will not be prepared. We must be patient and ever watchful or we may miss God's presence and be lost forever.

Advent is a time when we wait. We wait for the coming of the Lord in history, but we also wait for his coming at the end of time. The first event allows us time to prepare; the second requires constant vigilance. On this First Sunday of Advent, the parable of the doorkeeper challenges us to be watchful and prepare now, for we do not know the day or the hour.

Points Of Challenge And Questions To Ponder

1. How do we wait for the Lord? Many people wait with fear and apprehension about many things over which they have no control. If we do our best, as broken and incomplete as we are, to prepare now for Jesus' coming at the end of time, there is no need to be fearful or worry. We must take make every effort to respond to God's call now so that if the Lord's arrival is forecast we need change nothing in our lives.

2. What is our state of readiness for the Parousia? The belief that one is invincible, a "disease" that often plagues youth, is unfortunately present with many people. We think that tomorrow will come as assuredly as the sun will rise. Such an attitude does not allow one to prepare for the coming of the Lord.

3. Is my trust in God sufficiently strong that I can demonstrate patience in my day-to-day actions? Patience is a virtue which for many does not come easily. As the expression goes, "Grant me patience, Lord, and give it to me today!" Being patient is an important form of watchfulness; it says that we are prepared now, but can wait until the Lord comes.

4. What responsibility do we have to assist others in their readiness for the Lord? Discipleship asks many things of us, including the need to be evangelists. We cannot be satisfied that we have prepared ourselves and left others to their own devices. If we have the ability to be present, to give advice, to assist people in their daily preparation for the Lord, then as God's people we must so act.

5. What preparations are necessary in my life to be fully ready for the coming of the Lord? We all need to take the sometimes perilous yet always necessary journey of introspection. Who am I and what does God ask of me? If God calls me this day am I ready, or is there unfinished business to which I must attend? We must do our best to feel secure in the presence of the Lord each day of our lives.

Exegesis And Explanation Of The Parable

Chapter 13 of Mark's Gospel is known as the apocalyptic or eschatological discourse. It is the only place in this, the first Gospel to be written, where Jesus delivers a long consecutive teaching on a single subject. This chapter uses two forms of literary genre, apocalypse and farewell discourse. These styles were familiar to the people of the day and would have allowed them to understand the Lord's teaching fully. Mark 13 combines these two literary constructs as Jesus' final exhortation before the narrative recounts the Lord's passion, death, and resurrection. Apocalypse was a literary construct, very popular and widespread with the Jews between 200 B.C.E. and 200 C.E., in which an author revealed the substance of visions which had been granted him or her. Readers understood these visions as a picture of contemporary life or impending events. Apocalyptic literature was a means of sustaining hope and perseverance among an oppressed people in a time of imminent danger, downfall, or ruin. Readers were encouraged to believe that if apocalyptic prophecies of disaster, such as those proclaimed by the prophet Daniel, had been fulfilled, then the forecast of subsequent salvation would also come to pass.

Farewell discourses were another common literary model. Great religious leaders of the past, such as Jacob, Moses, Samuel, and David, when they knew they were about to die, summoned their family, disciples, or subjects and delivered to them what today would amount to a last will and testament. Such a speech might include past lessons, but it also proclaimed a summary of future prospects, especially forecasts of danger and suffering. Hearers of such an exhortation were advised to remain faithful through all future trials. A survey of the future was, like apocalyptic literature, believed to be based upon divine revelation. Thus, what was said was built on solid ground and could be used to warn, admonish, and instruct.

Mark's eschatological discourse seeks to explain to his readers what Jesus, in his capacity as the Son of Man, means for Jerusalem, for Christian disciples, and for all people. The evangelist uses the apocalyptic genre at this stage in his Gospel to highlight the divine vindication that Jesus will experience in the future. Mark cautions his readers to read the signs of the times (vv. 3-8) and forecasts future persecution (vv. 9-13) and the coming of the Son of Man (vv. 24-27). The chapter serves to balance his rather stark portrayal of the earthly sufferings of Jesus by widening the horizons of the reader to the positive results which his passion and death will bring to the world. The events related in this eschatological discourse thus provide Mark a means to describe God's final saving intervention in history.

Mark 13 closes with two parables, the image of the fig tree and the figure of the doorkeeper. While Jesus uses the fig tree to teach a lesson on recognizing the time when the Lord will return, the parable of the doorkeeper more specifically exhorts all to be watchful and wait for the coming of the Lord in the face of opposition from the world. Mark's readers certainly understood the parable to be an allegory: Christ is the departing Lord; the Parousia will mark his return. The doorkeeper represents the waiting disciples and the community of faith. The divisions of the night symbolize the lapses of time before the second advent of the Lord. The parable was most likely addressed to the scribes, who claimed to possess the keys of the kingdom of heaven. This is a "crisis" parable which the primitive Church applied to its own situation, perceiving itself between the crises of the Lord's death and the destruction of Jerusalem. The idea of watchfulness and vigilance was, therefore, clearly relevant to the people who first read Mark's words. The doorkeeper must watch *now* in order to be ready when the contemporary coincides with the future at the moment of Christ's return. The repeated call to watchfulness in verses 33, 35, and 37 indicates how Mark wanted not only the parable, but the whole eschatological discourse to be understood — not as a guide in calculating the time of Jesus' return, but as an invitation and a warning to live one's life at each moment in preparation for our future meeting with the Lord. This personal exhortation by Mark enhances the validity of the entire discourse.

The parable of the doorkeeper contains passages which have challenged scholars for generations. Verse 32, "But about that day or hour no one knows, neither the angels in heaven, nor the Son, but only the Father," reveals Mark's understanding of Jesus, not that defined at Chalcedon in 451. Some try to explain the verse by appealing to the communicative knowledge that Jesus (the Son) has for his mission, but this idea arises from a perspective that is not that of the evangelist. In its Marcan context the verse simply means that although the Parousia is imminent its precise date in not known. Scholars argue over the authenticity of Jesus' words.

Some believe that no Christian would be so bold as to place limits on Christ while others doubt Jesus ever referred to himself absolutely as the Son. (There is no parallel in Mark and only one doubtful reference in the other Synoptics, Matthew 11:27 and Luke 10:22.) Verse 37, "And what I say to you I say to all," lifts the whole discourse beyond the limits of the narrow perspective of the crisis of the day, the impending capture of Jerusalem and destruction of the Temple, and makes it applicable to all. Concluding in this manner, Mark thus makes universal the discourse and by extension the whole of Jesus' teaching.

Context Of The Parable

Context In The Church Year

In the life of the Church, our celebration of the First Sunday of Advent marks New Year's Day. As the first liturgical season, Advent provides many opportunities for renewal and hope. We generally think of Advent as the time which precedes Christmas and thus prepare for the Lord's coming in history. This is certainly true, but the season is twofold: a preparation for the Incarnation and for the Parousia, the second coming of the Lord. The preparations we make for Jesus' arrival on Christmas Day are different than those necessary for the Parousia. We know with certainty when Christmas will come and thus there is no great sense of urgency; we can procrastinate if we wish. Preparation for the Lord's second coming is very different. Scripture tells us that this event will come, but we have no idea when it will occur. Thus, a greater sense of vigilance is required; we must always be ready.

On the First Sunday of Advent the Church chooses readings which concentrate on this second theme of watchfulness and preparation. We begin a new liturgical year by reflecting upon the ultimate reason for our existence, the journey back to God. We do not like to think about death; it leaves a bad taste in our mouth. Yet, it is only through death that the great Christian paradox, that eternal life comes through death, can be experienced. We remember Jesus' words: "Unless a grain of wheat falls into the earth and dies, it remains just a single grain; but if it dies, it bears much fruit" (John

12:24). In order to appreciate fully the significance and power of the Incarnation, the Church asks us to consider our mortality and need for God while exhorting us to vigilance and preparedness in our day-to-day Christian journey. The parable of the doorkeeper challenges us to wait patiently and be ever watchful for Jesus' coming, for we do not know the day or the hour.

Context With Other Gospels

The parable of the doorkeeper is contained in different versions in all the Synoptic Gospels. The presence of this pericope in all three books demonstrates much more than a common source. Clearly the apostolic Church considered the exhortation to watchfulness to be of primary importance. Application of this parable to the entire Christian community has made its imprint in the text of all three Synoptic authors.

Matthew (25:14-15b) and Luke (19:12-13) cast the parable in a different light than Mark. These two evangelists speak of a master who entrusts his servants with his goods, goes on a journey, and when he returns, judges their accountability. The exhortation to watchfulness, which Mark connects to the master's journey, serves Matthew (24:42 and 25:13) and Luke (12:38) as an addendum to other teachings. Although the placement, method of presentation, and purpose of the basic parable differs for the three evangelists, all highlight the application of watchfulness as an immediate need for all disciples of Christ.

Context With First And Second Lessons

First Lesson: Isaiah 64:1-9. Writing to the Hebrews after their return from exile, Isaiah recaps his understanding of Israel's relationship with Yahweh and how it has been experienced in the past several generations. The prophet tells the people that God is their Father, but Israel strayed and hardened its heart against the Lord. Realizing their guilt, the people have now returned to the Lord and God has rescued them from the Babylonians. Isaiah tells the people that God will act for those who have the courage to wait. Patience and the ability to persevere will lead to deeds and wonders that no person has heard or seen.

The prophet's exhortation to the people to be patient and allow God to act coincides closely with the Lord's call to watchfulness in the parable of the doorkeeper. At times we all become frustrated at what we perceive to be the tardiness or failure of the Lord to respond to our prayers and petitions. We know, however, that God does not act on human time. The need to be ready and watchful must thus be united with the ability to be patient and allow God to act. In our ability to wait we find strength, and while we wait God hones and refines us, molding us to be the vessels that can better serve his divine plan.

Second Lesson: 1 Corinthians 1:3-9. Saint Paul, like Isaiah with the Hebrews, exhorts the Christian community at Corinth to wait patiently for the revelation of Jesus Christ in the Parousia. Christ's coming in glory and power was a cardinal doctrine of Saint Paul's preaching and the main object of Christian hope. Paul speaks of how our faithful God has called us to fellowship with Christ. Thus, when the Lord returns those who have been faithful, patient, and observant of his teachings will reap a great reward. As with Isaiah and Mark's parable, Paul clearly teaches that a life of vigilance, watchfulness, and patience will be rewarded with the eternal presence of God.

Chapter 2

Living For Others

John 10:11-18

---

*"I am the good shepherd. The good shepherd lays down
his life for the sheep. The hired hand, who is not the
shepherd and does not own the sheep, sees the wolf
coming and leaves the sheep and runs away — and the
wolf snatches them and scatters them. The hired hand
runs away because a hired hand does not care for the
sheep. I am the good shepherd. I know my own and my
own know me, just as the Father knows me and I know
the Father. And I lay down my life for the sheep. I have
other sheep that do not belong to this fold. I must bring
them also, and they will listen to my voice. So there
will be one flock, one shepherd. For this reason the
Father loves me, because I lay down my life in order to
take it up again. No one takes it from me, but I lay it
down of my own accord. I have power to lay it down,
and I have power to take it up again. I have received
this command from my Father."*

Theme

Discipleship, the daily walk in the footsteps of Jesus, is both a
privilege and a challenge. To have the opportunity to assist the
Son of God in his work to reclaim the world for the Father should
make all people feel wonderful and empower them to seek great
heights in their daily endeavors. Yet we know that it is not easy to
be a disciple; the road we walk is often strewn with many obstacles
that are difficult to negotiate. The image of Jesus as the Good

Shepherd brings encouragement amidst the sea of despair in contemporary life. Jesus' selfless action of laying down his life for all people strenghtens our determination to continue walking the road, following the one whose life we seek to imitate and whose presence in heaven we desire.

Spiritual Food For The Journey

The Good Shepherd, Jesus Christ, our brother, friend, and Lord, beckons us to walk in his footsteps. In order to follow Jesus we must be willing to sacrifice, to live more fully for others in all that we say and do. Discipleship, living for others, begins with an attitude. First, we must treat all people with human dignity. We are called to care for our brothers and sisters with respect and love. Secondly, we must treat all people equally. Race, religion, sex, creed — these should have no bearing on the way we understand and receive others. We are all brothers and sisters, children of God, who are equal in God's eyes. Lastly, we must show fraternity in our relationship with one another. Living in community, sharing our lives, thoughts and prayers — this is being fraternal, this is living for others.

Living for others continues with our actions. Through our common baptismal call we are asked to lead lives of service, especially to the poor and those who have little or no voice in our world. We are challenged to lead lives of ministry. It may be formal ministry as a full-time person at a parish or church-related organization. For most, however, our lives of ministry are less formal, but equally important. In the church we live for others by ministry, through our participation in the liturgical celebration, efforts to assist the poor, and other service-related projects and organizations. In the community we live for others through local government, fraternal organizations, and volunteer work. Living lives of self-giving and sacrifice — this is ministry. Parents living for their children, families visiting elder members in hospitals and nursing homes, people giving their time and talent so others may share their abundance — these are all examples of living for others. This is participating in the divine.

Jesus, our brother, friend, and Lord, lived totally for others. Jesus freely laid down his life for us. Why? Because he loved us and wanted to share himself with us. Jesus the Good Shepherd asks us to live our lives in a similar manner. Jesus asks us to live for others in attitude, in word, and in action. Jesus asks us to love, especially those we find most difficult to love. Jesus asks us to lay down our lives, through service, ministry, and sacrifice. If we live for others, if we love, if we lay down our lives, then we participate in the divinity of Jesus and make the resurrection a reality in contemporary society.

Application Of The Parable To Contemporary Life

Sermon Openings
1. How does one define the concept of divinity? We might begin by some description of the aspects of being divine. The divine is infinite; the divine is omnipotent and omniscient. These ideas help to describe divinity, but they don't do much to define it. We need something to which we can relate so as to understand the concept of the divine.

The best answer to our original question for me is to speak in terms of participation in the divine. Thus, one can ask the question, how can one seek to be divine-like? An answer which appeals to me is — to the degree that we live for others is the degree to which we participate in the divine. We can give many examples of this idea. There is a dramatic example in the life of Saint Maximilian Kolbe. Kolbe was a Franciscan friar who ministered as a publisher and writer. He was sent to the Auschwitz death camp during World War II. There he laid down his life, volunteering to die for another prisoner, who happened to be a family man. Another dramatic example is one I saw on television many years ago. In the so-called "Ironman" competition held annually in Hawaii, where one swims two miles, bikes over 150 miles, and then finishes with a 26.2 mile marathon run, one competitor participated in and finished the race with his crippled son strapped to his back. He ran, biked, and swam for his son.

There are more famous examples of living for others. In his "I have a dream" speech presented on the Washington Mall in August 1963, Martin Luther King, Jr., expressed the hopes which he shared and lived for in creating a more just world for all. John F. Kennedy, in his inaugural address said, "Ask not what your country can do for you, ask what you can do for your country."

There are incalculable routine and ordinary ways in which people live for others, yet maybe they are the most profound because they are everyday events. People who donate time to work in a soup line, a youngster who shares her sandwich with a child who has none, parents who sacrifice time, energy, and resources out of love for their children. To the extent that we live for others is the extent to which we participate in the divine.

Jesus was divine and thus he lived totally for others. In the Gospel we hear a familiar story and a powerful image of Jesus as the Good Shepherd who lays down his life for others.

2. "When Christ calls a man, he bids him come and die." These words of Dietrich Bonhoeffer, the famous Lutheran theologian and pastor, challenge our world and its sensibility. The words were written in 1937 in a book which has been influential in the life of many, including myself, *The Cost of Discipleship*. As his words suggest, the cost of following Jesus, the cost of discipleship, is very high — in fact, it will cost us our very lives.

Most people do not want to think about the cost of following the Lord. To think of the cost may be very frightening. The cost of following the Lord, the cost of discipleship, may be more than we are willing or able to pay. Dietrich Bonhoeffer knew the cost of discipleship; he paid the ultimate price. During the period of Nazi rule in Germany Bonhoeffer spoke out against the tyranny, the anti-Semitism, the insanity. He was imprisoned and eventually executed shortly before the end of the World War II by executive order of Heinrich Himmler on April 9, 1945.

Calculating the cost of discipleship, the cost of following Christ, is something each Christian is called to do. The movie *Field of Dreams*, produced several years ago, well illustrates this need in our lives. In the movie we are introduced to a family who lives in the Midwest. The parents are products of the Berkeley free-speech movement of the 1960s. They raise corn on a medium-sized farm. One day while walking in his cornfield, the father of the family hears a soft voice say to him, "If you build it, they will come." The voice speaks to the man several times over a long period of time. Eventually, the father comes to realize that the mysterious voice is referring to "Shoeless" Joe Jackson, a famous baseball player from the past, who was a favorite of the man. If the father, who is a great sports fan, will build a baseball field, Joe will come and play.

The man and his wife sit down and calculate the outlay. They make a plan to follow in order to build the field for Shoeless Joe and his teammates. They are forewarned of future problems. Their neighbors criticize them; they think it crazy to build a baseball field in the middle of a cornfield. Still, the couple understands the price that they must pay; they are willing to accept the cost. In the end the field is built, the players come, and the farm survives. The faith of the man in listening to the soft and mysterious voice made it all possible. The cost was high but the rewards were even greater.

Our Gospel today combines the words of Dietrich Bonhoeffer and the message of *Field of Dreams* and challenges us to ask, how much are we willing to pay to follow the Lord?

Points Of Challenge And Questions To Ponder

1. Is discipleship a non-negotiable aspect of our lives? Are our actions and words directed toward our overall efforts to walk in the footsteps of the Lord?

2. When people observe and hear us, what is the image they receive? Do they observe a good shepherd who works tirelessly for others, sacrificing self for the betterment of the whole?

3. Has the resurrection transformed us to a belief in the need for greater care for others? Can we live more fully for others in the small as well as the grand tasks of daily life?

4. Is our attitude in dealing with associates, neighbors, colleagues at work one of inclusivity or exclusivity? Are we welcoming in our words and actions? Do others feel comfortable seeking assistance from us or do they receive the "cold shoulder"?

5. How have we been doing in our tasks of caring for those whom God has given to us? Do we take our responsibility of being caregivers seriously? Can others count on us to "be there" for them or are people often disappointed in us and our lack of trustworthiness?

Exegesis And Explanation Of The Parable

Scholars debate how this famous passage of the Good Shepherd was created. Some see 10:1-5 as a parable and 10:7-18 as the parable's allegorical and perhaps secondary explanation. Proponents of this belief see this pericope as analogous to the relationship of the parable of the sower, Mark 4:1-9 and its interpretation in 4:13-20. There are several problems with this understanding, however. First, there is no one-to-one correspondence between figures in verses 1-5 and Jesus' words in verses 7-18. Many of the elements of the so-called parable, such as the gatekeeper and stranger, are ignored and new figures, the hired hand and wolf, introduced. Jesus uses pastoral imagery in verses 7-18, but its purpose is to move in a new direction.

Some scholars suggest a better comparsion of verses 7-18 is to the imagery of John chapter 6. In this chapter a series of "I am" statements is followed by theological expansion (6:35 with 36-40, 6:41 with 43-47, and 6:48 with 49-50). In John 6 Jesus' self-revelation is couched in language and images from the exodus tradition to demonstrate that Jesus is the true fulfillment of Moses' hopes. A similar use of language and imagery is at work in John 10:7-18. In reworking the Old Testament pastoral imagery, Jesus shows how he is the one who meets the needs of the sheep.

The image of the shepherd, central to this pericope, has been used in many ways in ancient writings. In Oriental and Greek antiquity, literature often compared a ruler with the shepherd and the people with the flock. In the Hebrew Scriptures the image of the shepherd is quite common. Prophets like Moses and kings like David are called good shepherds and the evil leaders of the people are referred to as bad shepherds. Israel is often described as the flock. The most important Old Testament image of the Good Shepherd is found in Ezekiel 34. Here Yahweh stongly condemns the rulers of Israel as tyrannous and negligent shepherds who have grossly abused their office, feeding themselves instead of the sheep. Now the hour of righteous judgment has come and Yahweh will intervene. The unworthy shepherds will be deposed and God will become personally responsible for the care of the sheep. Most Scripture experts agree that Ezekiel 34 was used as a source for the whole of John 10:1-21.

The image of the shepherd in the New Testament is largely dependent on Old Testament ideas. The idea of sheep without a shepherd of Mark 6:34 and Matthew 9:36 is found in Numbers 27:17. Mark 14:27, the shepherd who will be struck down, echoes Zechariah 13:7, where the death of the shepherd is necessary so that the flock may be purified. In his Messianic rule Jesus is referred to as the shepherd in 1 Peter 2:25, alluding to Isaiah 35:6 (as well as New Testament references Hebrews 13:20 and 1 Peter 5:4). The shepherd Messiah of Revelation 12:5 and 19:15 is found in Psalm 2:9.

The image of the shepherd in John 10, although in some ways corresponding to Old Testament images, is generally unique in its presentation. In John, as in the Hebrew Scriptures, the shepherd leads the flock (v. 4), guides it to pasture (v. 9), and protects the sheep from wolves (vv. 11-13). In John, however, there is no idea of the shepherd as a Messianic or kingly figure. Equally important is that the flock is not Israel, but his "own." John's idea of the reciprocal relationship between the shepherd and the sheep, described in the shepherd's call and the sheep hearing his voice (vv. 3-4), is absent in the Old Testament. These facts lead most scholars to conclude that the Johannine shepherd is either an original concept or is drawn from another tradition. Some exegetes suggest that the Gnostic tradition and its *Mandaean* literature is the source of this image, although others believe the ideas are original to John.

The Good Shepherd image is contrasted with the character of the hireling. The latter is portrayed in a totally negative light; he fails in his duty in times of danger. Similar images of a hireling as a poor shepherd are found in Ezekiel 34:5-6, 8-10, Jeremiah 23:1-3, and Zechariah 11:15, 17. The hired hand has no relationship with the sheep but rather works solely for pay and security. If this passage has any polemical overtones, then those Jews opposed to Jesus and the Christian community may be the ones singled out by John for condemnation. The Good Shepherd is portrayed as the one who loves and cares for the sheep. This Christological metaphor became a powerful and favorite symbol for Christians in the apostolic and Patristic periods.

The idea of the Good Shepherd who lays down his life for the flock is another critical aspect of the Johannine image. Although Palestinian shepherding practices may have called for a significant commitment, even to death, to the sheep, John's way of presenting this idea is so distinctive that the reader cannot help but hear in Jesus' words an allusion to his own death. Jesus' selfless act of love manifests the high point of his relationship with his flock, the people. For the simple yet profound reason that he knows and loves them, Jesus stakes the ultimate on their behalf. John makes it unmistakably clear that the Good Shepherd is voluntarily laying down his life in loving fulfillment and obedience to the Father's will. Jesus is the Suffering Servant of Isaiah 53:10-12 whose life is offered for the ransom of many. The evangelist wants his readers to understand that we are not to see Jesus as a shepherd and true ruler of his people who happens to lay down his life, but rather as the true ruler of God's people **only because he freely chooses** to sacrifice himself. Jesus' selfless action is part of his office; his reign in part consists of self-offering for those who govern. Through all of this Jesus remains as the servant of all.

A related idea to Jesus' self-sacrifice is its connection to the resurrection and obedience to the Father. In verses 17 and 18 Jesus mentions the unquestioned fact that the Father loves the Son in order to place context on the forthcoming events. In stating that he will lay down his life to take it up again, Jesus is demonstrating that the resurrection follows of necessity upon his self-sacrifice and, in fact, is intended to go with it. Jesus' death and resurrection are both part of the Father's mandate. Thus, the Lord fulfills God's promise as he does the Father's will. Jesus is the Good Shepherd not simply because of his relationship with the sheep but also because of his relationship with his Father.

Verses 17 and 18 focus on three important theological themes. First, Jesus' death is placed fully in the context of his relationship with the Father. Second, Jesus' free choice to lay down his life is an expression of obedience to God. Christ is not a victim in death, not a martyr, but rather has control of his destiny. Lastly, these verses point to the inseparability of Jesus' death and resurrection in the Johannine corpus. Jesus' work to build the Kingdom of God is incomplete until he returns to the Father through his resurrection and ascension. These verses point to the complete union of God and Jesus, a union which becomes explicit in 10:30: "The Father and I are one."

This passage in John's Gospel presents another new and important teaching on the universality of the Christian message. Verse 16 challenges the familiar eschatological expectation that only the twelve tribes of Israel will be gathered together from their diaspora state and reunited. Here John expresses the idea that the children of God will be gathered together under the one shepherd, Jesus Christ. Judaism, the religion of the chosen people, has been universalized; God's call is now proclaimed to all people. This new community of God will grow, while remaining undivided, into a single people in which the "other sheep" will not only be tolerated as late arrivals, but viewed as a gift. This verse is understood to be a very short summary of the central message of Romans 9-11, where Paul speaks of the Jews' rejection of the Messiah and the subsequent opportunity of salvation given to the Gentiles.

The shepherd discourse in John 10:11-18 provides the contemporary church with the opportunity to reflect on certain critical theological concepts. The church is first asked to attend to the Christological heart of its identity. The identity of the church cannot be separated from the identity of Jesus; it is thus inextricably linked to the Christological conversation. Secondly, this passage provides the opportunity to reassess the assumptions that accompany the use of shepherd and pastoral imagery with respect to church leaders. Finally, this discourse provides the church with a fresh vantage point from which to reflect on community practices. What responsibility do individual Christians have to live as Jesus' sheep? This passage challenges the Christian community to live out its life according to the model of community envisioned here by Jesus, a model grounded in the mutuality of love embodied in the relationship of Jesus and God.

Context Of The Parable

Context In The Church Year

The Easter season is an appropriate time to hear the message of the Good Shepherd. As the Good Shepherd, Jesus provides the perfect example of discipleship, a message that is clear, unmistakable, and universal. Self-sacrifice and obedience to the will of God are key elements of the role of any true disciple. The Good Shepherd posseses these attributes and exercises them for the benefit of his sheep. The resurrection of Jesus was the Lord's triumph over death that brought the possibility of eternal life to all people. In describing how the Good Shepherd has many flocks that he tends, the universality of the resurrection message is made clear. Christianity seeks to be inclusive, not exclusive. The actions of the Good Shepherd give us assurance of God's care for us. Rejoicing in the resurrection, we can simultaneously take consolation in God's abiding presence in our lives.

Context With Other Gospels

The image of the Good Shepherd is unique to John's Gospel. As described above, the Synoptics contain references to Israel as sheep and the concept of a shepherd as ruler, but the self-sacrificing nature of the Johannine image of Christ as the Good Shepherd illustrates the understanding of a shepherd in a new light. As with the whole of the fourth Gospel, this passage provides special insight and theological perspective. The necessity of Christ's sacrifice and eventual triumph over death and the universality of the

Lord's call are critical aspects that make this passage significant for all Christians for all time.

Context With First And Second Lessons

First Lesson: Acts 4:5-12. Saint Peter was a man who was truly transformed by the resurrection. Before Christ's triumph over the grave Peter is portrayed by the Gospel evangelists as one who misunderstands, says the wrong things, is fearful, and most importantly denies the Lord three times in Christ's greatest hour of need. After the resurrection, however, Peter is a new man. He energetically goes forward and proclaims Jesus' message with no fear of the consequences of his actions. In this passage from the Acts of the Apostles Peter tells those assembled that it is his faith in Christ which allows him to heal others. There is no salvation in anyone but Jesus. He accuses the Jews of rejecting Jesus, the cornerstone.

Jesus, the Good Shepherd, showed us how to live for others. Peter, as a true disciple, took Jesus' words and actions to heart, transformed his life, and began to live for others. In curing the cripple he assisted an individual; in speaking out and announcing why he was able to perform a cure he broadcasts Jesus' universal message of love. We are encouraged to demonstrate discipleship, in imitation of Jesus and Peter.

Second Lesson: 1 John 3:16-24. Saint John's first epistle mirrors many of the themes of his Gospel. The concepts of discipleship and self-sacrifice illustrated by the Good Shepherd are present in this passage. John says that we come to understand love in observing Christ's selfless action in laying down his life for us. John goes on to challenge his readers to love in action and not merely to talk about it. We are only able to perform such service and be disciples by keeping focused on Christ and his command to love.

Discipleship lived well is never an easy road. The apostles knew this fact well; we should not be surprised. Encouraged by the example of Saint John and his inspiring words in this passage, we are armed and ready for future battles, doing our best to demonstrate our faith in Jesus, the one whom we serve.

Chapter 3

Union With God
And God's People

John 15:1-8

---

*"I am the true vine, and my Father is the vinegrower.
He removes every branch in me that bears no fruit.
Every branch that bears fruit he prunes to make it bear
more fruit. You have already been cleansed by the word
that I have spoken to you. Abide in me as I abide in
you. Just as the branch cannot bear fruit by itself unless it abides in the vine, neither can you unless you
abide in me. I am the vine, you are the branches. Those
who abide in me and I in them bear much fruit, because apart from me you can do nothing. Whoever does
not abide in me is thrown away like a branch and with-
ers; such branches are gathered, thrown into the fire,
and burned. If you abide in me, and my words abide in
you, ask for whatever you wish, and it will be done for
you. My Father is glorified by this, that you bear much
fruit and become my disciples."*

Theme

We often hear the expression, "With God all things are possible." As God's children we have many hopes and dreams — for
ourselves and those we love and respect. We want the best for
those we know, but we realize there may be some price to pay for
all that we desire. The cost, however, cannot be measured in mon-
etary ways, because what we must do is merely maintain the con-

nection that already exists between us and God. Through baptism we have been united with God, but as life progresses we may move away from the source of our strength, from the one who provides for us and all those we know. Our need for Christ is paramount; we cannot survive without him. In the figure of the vine and the branches we are challenged to renew our commitment, to reconnect ourselves to the source of eternal life.

Spiritual Food For The Journey

Unity versus disunity — these words are more than mere opposites. Certainly when unity exists things are together; where disunity reigns things are apart. There is more, however, to understanding these terms. Unity is something that is quite natural; it is the natural flow of nature, for humans and the world in general. Unity is something we seek; it does our world good to discover unity. Disunity, on the other hand, is seldom found in nature. Disunity is unnatural and not desired by humans; disunity is to be avoided.

Since unity is that which we desire, we need to find images that help us to picture this idea. One good example is alloy metals. An alloy is a mixture of two dissimilar metals which when molded together form a third metal which is stronger, longer-lasting, and more durable than either of the original two metals from which it is made. Energy is needed to bind the metals is this newly found unity. Rivers are another example of the unity in nature. Tributaries of a river flow into the whole. The larger river is stronger, deeper, and more useful than the tributaries from which it is formed. The boundaries of the river, its banks, hold it together, allowing it to flow freely and sustain much life in the process.

Humans seek unity as well. The peoples of nations seek unity. We live in the United States, a nation of fifty independent sovereigns or states, yet these independent states choose to band together as one. What binds them together is the law of the land, the Constitution. In the United States the charism of the Declaration of Independence, which says "all people are created equal," serves to bind us together. Humans band together in communities as well.

It may be a neighborhood watch group or a community action organization. It may even be a religious community of men or women. The bond here is the common issue, the common commitment, or the common way of life.

The figure of the vine and the branches demonstrates our need to be united with Christ. Disunity, separation from the vine, will produce no yield. We must be connected with Christ to gain the strength we need to live in our world. By our maintenance of union with Christ and the combining of our efforts to those of the entire Christian community we will bear much fruit and one day find eternal life.

Application Of The Parable To Contemporary Life

Sermon Openings
1. "Outlined against a blue-gray October sky, the Four Horsemen rode again. In dramatic lore they are known as pestilence, famine, destruction, and death. These are only aliases. There real names are Stuhldreher, Miller, Layden, and Crowley." Grantland Rice, a well-known sports columnist in an earlier era, wrote those memorable words one Saturday in October 1927. With these words a legend was started, for Notre Dame football, the team's immortal coach Knute Rockne, and, that day especially, for the Four Horsemen of Notre Dame.

Who were the Four Horsemen? Elmer Layden, Harry Stuhldreher, Jim Crowley, and Don Miller were the talented offensive backfield for the Notre Dame football team in the late 1920s. There is no doubt that they were great players. Football fans then and now remember their names and their exploits on the gridiron. All four have been enshrined in the College Football Hall of Fame.

Most people know, however, that there are eleven players on a football team. What about the other seven? Who were they? What did they do? History knows them as the "Seven Mules." Few, if anyone, remember their names. None of them are members of the College Football Hall of Fame. Still, I am certain that the Four Horsemen knew them. In fact, the same Grantland Rice who immortalized the horsemen said that this talented backfield attributed all their success to the mules. They were the ones who stood in front, did the blocking, ran interference, and paved a way for the two halfbacks, the fullback, and quarterback to run the plays, score touchdowns, and bring victory to Notre Dame.

The Four Horsemen and the Seven Mules were a team; they knew that they needed each other. Without the mules the horsemen probably would have been an ordinary college football backfield. But the combination of the mules and the horsemen brought greatness, fame, and legend to Miller, Layden, Crowley, and Stuhldreher and to Notre Dame football as well.

I am reminded of this idea of teamwork, players who need each other, when I hear today's Gospel. Jesus says that we need to be teammates with him, "for apart from him we can do nothing."

2. "Late have I loved you, O Beauty so ancient and so new, late have I loved you." These famous words come from an equally famous book. It was written after a life of trial, searching, and change. They were written by one who had found conversion in his life. He was born in Thagaste, now the country of Algeria, in the year 354. His father was Patricius, a Roman citizen and pagan. His mother was Monica, a prayerful Christian woman of simple means.

It was clear to all from his earliest days that he possessed great gifts, especially intellectually. Yet he seemed to live his life as an individual; he was quite self-centered. All of life was for him, his projects, his education, his welfare. As a young man he was a teacher of rhetoric. He became well-known for his intelligence and probing mind.

Despite fame and success, his life of "individualism" lacked something. The void he felt was community; he needed the presence of others and he needed God. Thus he began to search for that which was missing in his life — his need for community and God. Pagan religions offered no help to this man of great intelligence and erudition. Manichaeism, a sect which was centered about the dualism of good and evil, attracted him, but after a few years his dissatisfaction returned. Finally, he answered the call to Christianity. He found people and community; he discovered God. He learned that the world was not me, the world is us!

48

"Late have I loved you, O Beauty so ancient and so new." These words are found in the *Confessions*, the autobiography of Saint Augustine, bishop of Hippo, one of the most gifted and famous men who ever lived. Augustine was a man who experienced the call to conversion and change in his life.

In the figure of the vine and the branches we are challenged to consider our need for God. We must ponder our need to better appreciate God's power and wonder as manifest to us in the lives of those we know and love.

Points Of Challenge And Questions To Ponder

1. Do we place our hope and reliance on Jesus or do we seek other sources to the solutions of our problems? Are people and material "fixes" more attractive than our union with Christ?

2. Do we "go it alone"? Are we people who say, "I will do my own thing"? Do we consider the needs and feelings of others in our decisions?

3. Is the Christian community important to us? Do we make efforts to contribute to the whole or are we more concerned with meeting our own needs?

4. Are we team players or do we refuse to participate in the activities of the community? Can we trust others to assist us, or do we shut out others, believing that the job can only be satisfactorily completed by ourselves?

5. When we minister in the name of the Lord do we do so as individuals or as a community? Can we believe in the power and strength of union with the whole compared with our individual efforts? Do we perceive and believe in our need for one another?

Exegesis And Explanation Of The Parable

Beginning with the thirteenth chapter, John's Gospel takes a significant shift in its orientation. Prior to this point Jesus' hour has been anticipated (2:4, 7:30, 8:20) or acknowledged as imminent (12:33, 27), but 13:1 signals its arrival. The occurrences narrated in John 13:1—17:26 are situated at the Last Supper where three major events transpire: the washing of the apostles' feet and subsequent dialogues between Jesus and his disciples (13:1-38); the farewell discourse (14:1—16:33); and Jesus' prayer (17:1-26). The metaphor of the vine and the branches, John 15:1-8, is part of the Lord's last teaching to his followers. It stands, therefore, as Jesus' last testament on how he expected his disciples to conduct their lives. Rather than an indictment against individuals or groups for wrongdoing or an exhortation to conversion, this pericope is Jesus' explanation of how people will find life after he has gone. It is appropriate that Jesus' final lesson emphasizes the recipe for eternal life.

Chapter 15 as a literary whole encourages the disciples to make their unity with Jesus fruitful and to endure the hostility of the world. In this chapter Jesus continues his farewell discourse, transferring it to the sphere of the community by applying the Lord's words to all. This discourse is not for the apostles alone; John is writing for all believers. Most biblical exegetes regard John 15:1-17 as a single connected discourse. Here John speaks of the relationship of Christians to Christ, the community of life they share, and the need for Christ as a source for the good works of all believers. In verses 1-8 we are introduced to the image of the vine. This metaphor presupposes that the Christian life is essentially one of activity and of bearing fruit. Union with Christ is not only the condition of bearing fruit; our activity in Jesus' name demands such a connection. Verses 9-17 are centered about the need for the apostles to demonstrate love in all aspects of their lives. The exposition of the command to love as the essential element of faith makes it quite clear that faith and love form a unity. Verses 1-8 exhort us to renew our connection to Jesus, while verses 9-17 command love in response to our God who first loved us.

The vocabulary of 15:1-8, the metaphor of the vine and the branches, is quite close to the *mashal* (Hebrew for riddle or figure of speech) used in Ezekiel 17. In order to understand this passage we must begin by describing what Jesus means when he identifies himself as the vine. Jesus as the true and authentic vine is contrasted with whatever claims to be the "vine." This discourse does not draw attention to the vine with regard to its fruit or to the wine that may be produced, but simply to the vine itself and the branches which derive their vital power from it. From the vine the branches receive their power to grow and to bear fruit. If the branches grow independently, they are cut away. In calling himself the true vine, Jesus is stating that no natural life is true. The life that humanity seeks and longs for can only be found in association with Jesus. The only true life is in God; all other forms are mundane or a lie. Jesus' self-identification as the vine is understood best in the context of his relationship with his community of followers. Thus, when Jesus spoke of himself as the vine, his words were not only self-revelatory, but revealed the interrelationship of God the Father, Jesus the Son, and the community of faith.

The basic meaning of the parable is quite clear. Just as Jesus is the source of living water (4:10, 14) and the bread from heaven that gives life (6:35), so he is the life-giving vine. Before the metaphor, those concerned with receiving the gift of Jesus' life needed external actions; one had to drink the water or eat the bread of life. The imagery of the vine is more intimate, as befits the general theme of interiorization in the farewell discourse. In order to have life one must remain in Jesus as a branch stays on the vine. In comparing himself to a vine and his disciples as branches, Jesus makes himself known not only as the sustainer but also as the origin and source of true life that may only be found through union with him.

The image of the vine and branches has certain distinctions that should be understood. One important feature is that there is nothing futuristic in the description of the union between the vine and the branches. In several other passages of the farewell discourse, union with Jesus is described as belonging to the future (14:3, 20-22, 16:22). In this pericope, however, the disciples are already in union with Jesus, with the emphasis placed on remaining in this union. Some scholars suggest that this pericope is misplaced in the Johannine redaction, that Jesus orginally spoke these words on the road between Bethany and Jerusalem in conjunction with the cursing of the fig tree. Biblical exegetes also see some allegory in this passage. The removal of the unfruitful branches has been suggested to be a reference to the defection of Judas as being typical for all faithless disciples. The nurturing of the branches is seen as allegory for the growth of the Christian community. The church exists to teach and evangelize, but in order to do this well it must receive pruning at the hands of God.

Some scholars perceive Eucharistic connotations in this metaphor. Since Jesus gave this teaching at the Last Supper some understand the "fruit of the vine" as a reference to the Eucharist, especially since John makes no specific reference to the sacrament's institution in his Gospel. Exegetes have compared 15:5, "I am the vine, you are the branches. Those who abide in me and I in them bear much fruit ..." with 6:56 (part of the Bread of Life Discourse); "Those who eat my flesh and drink my blood abide in me and I in them." An ancient tradition, now refuted, placed Jesus' metaphor of the vine and branches immediately after the distribution of the Eucharistic cup. Some scholars also point out that union with Christ in his death, central to our understanding of the Eucharist, is a central theme of the whole of chapter 15.

The image of community that emerges from this pericope is one of interrelationship, mutuality, and indwelling. In Jesus, the true vine, the life of God with the human race, the essence of Israel's true and desired existence has begun. The relationship of the vine to the branches conveys to the disciples a true sense of the profound intimacy of their relationship to Jesus Christ. Jesus had spoken of the intimacy of the disciples being in him and he in them. The metaphor of the vine and branches is an illustration of that intimacy. What the vine image suggests about community is that there are no free-standing individuals; all gain their origins, sustenance, and strength from the vine. The fruitfulness of each branch depends on its relationship to the vine, nothing else. What matters for John the evangelist is that each individual be rooted in Jesus, give up individual status, and become one of the true branches connected to the vine.

Context Of The Parable

Context In The Church Year

The Easter season is a time when we are challenged to renew our attitudes and review our actions. We reflect upon our own activities, efforts, and actions, but we must also be concerned about renewal of the whole Christian community. During this season we hear in our Sunday Scripture lessons about the early Christian community — their hopes, dreams, and struggles — as described by Saint Luke in the Acts of the Apostles. The story of the first followers of Jesus is inspiring in how they demonstrated true love for one another. They manifest this most basically in the way they lived as a community. The first Christians realized that the only way they could survive and grow was by working together. Community became a source of life for these people.

It is appropriate during this season of grace that the church provides Jesus' vivid image of the the vine and branches to remind us of our need for Christ and the church. United with Christ and combining our efforts with those of the Christian community as a whole will bring a rich harvest in God's kingdom. The church asks us through this metaphor of the vine and branches to renew our efforts to work together in building the Kingdom of God on earth.

Context With Other Gospels

The metaphor of the vine and branches is found only in the Gospel of John, but Scripture possesses many references to the image of the vineyard present in this pericope. The metaphor is prominent in both the Old and New Testamants. In the Hebrew Scriptures (Isaiah 5:1-7, Jeremiah 2:21, 12:10, Ezekiel 15:2-8, 19:10-14, and Hosea 10:1) the figure of the vine is descriptive of Israel as a nation. All these accounts picture the vine as a degenerate plant which has brought its sufferings upon itself. The parable of the wicked tenants (Matthew 21:33-46, Mark 12:1-12, and Luke 20:9-19) also illustrates the idea of the vineyard as representative of Israel. It is highly significant, therefore, that in the figure of the vine and the branches, Jesus applies this image to himself. The prophetic use of the image of the vine led to predictions of judgment and disaster. In stark contrast, Jesus uses the metaphor as the source and sustenance of life. In another context, some scholars have compared the figure of the vine and branches in John with the Pauline image of Christ as head of the body (1 Corinthians 12), although Paul's metaphor is more highly developed.

Context With First And Second Lessons
First Lesson: Acts 8:26-40. Philip's actions as an evangelist in this lesson from the Acts of the Apostles demonstrate the missionary spirit in the early church. The apostles and other disciples, filled with the Holy Spirit, demonstrated their connection to the vine that is Jesus. Philip knew that his strength to preach God's message, to know when to speak and what to say to the Ethopian eunuch, was gained from his relationship with Jesus. He understood that with Jesus he could bear fruit, but apart from him he could do nothing. It was through the relationship which Jesus established with his followers and his teaching in such passages as the metaphor of the vine and the branches that the apostolic Church found the courage, strength, and perseverance to proclaim the Good News, often in less than friendly environments. We are challenged to find our sustenance in Christ and fearlessly go forward to tell others of our brother, savior, and lord — Jesus Christ.

Second Lesson: 1 John 4:7-21. Saint John speaks of love as a response to God that finds its origins in our union with the Lord. He writes, "God is love, and those who abide in love abide in God, and God abides in them" (v. 16b). Love, the basic manifestation of Christ's message on earth, will be discovered by staying in communion with Jesus. John tells us that we have a great need for Christ; he is the source of our life each day. If we separate ourselves from Jesus our ability to love will be destroyed and so too will our relationship with God's people. In order to imitate the life of God we must learn to love more fully, for, as John says, love is of God.

Chapter 4

Jesus: The Victor Over Evil

Mark 3:20-35

The crowd came together again, so that they could not even eat. When his family heard it, they went out to restrain him, for people were saying, "He has gone out of his mind." And the scribes who came down from Jerusalem said, "He has Beelzebul, and by the ruler of the demons he casts out demons." And he called them to him, and spoke to them in parables. "How can Satan cast out Satan? If a kingdom is divided against itself, that kingdom cannot stand. And if a house is divided against itself, that house will not be able to stand. And if Satan has risen up against himself and is divided, he cannot stand, but his end has come. But no one can enter a strong man's house and plunder his prosperity without first tying up the strong man; then indeed the house can be plundered.

"Truly I tell you, people will be forgiven for their sins and whatever blasphemies they utter; but whoever blasphemes against the Holy Spirit can never have forgiveness, but is guilty of an eternal sin" — for they had said, "He has an unclean spirit."

Then his mother and his brothers came; and standing outside, they sent to him and called him. A crowd was sitting around him; and they said to him, "Your mother and your brothers and sisters are outside, asking for you." And he replied, "Who are my mother and my brothers?" And looking at those who sat around

him, he said, "Here are my mother and my brothers!
Whoever does the will of God is my brother and sister
and mother."

Theme

Years ago ABC's *Wide World of Sports* each Saturday would broadcast some event which demonstrated the program's motto "The thrill of victory and the agony of defeat." All people like to be winners, whether it is on the athletic field, the stock market, the gaming table, or a game of cards. Sometimes we experience how victory is snatched from the jaws of defeat. We hear about the baseball team that is down by three runs with two men out in the bottom of the ninth inning and manages to win. At the races it sometimes happens that the long shot, ten lengths back with a half mile to go, manages to sprint forward and break the tape, the winner.

Our world is often shrouded in the darkness of defeat. Problems, loss, feelings of guilt, defeat, and sadness tend to weigh us down. We might lose hope, but we know that Jesus, who triumphed over death itself, is here to set the tables straight. Our faith and the Scriptures assure us that Jesus is present and will ultimately bring us triumph, as he snatched victory from defeat in his salvific death. If we stay close to Christ, experience his power, and always do our best to be a team player, we too will experience victory and the reward of eternal life.

Spiritual Food For The Journey

Power is a concept which can be experienced in two different ways. The power of physical things is readily visible, measurable, and limited. Anyone who has been on a ship at sea, especially during a storm, knows that the ocean possesses great power. Ships of great tonnage are tossed about like plastic toy boats in a bathtub. Vehicles which move us from one place to another exhibit this same form of physical power. Rockets send satellites and humans into space; planes, trains, and automobiles carry us to and from work and recreation. The ocean and these vehicles each possess a measurable and limited amount of power which can be harnessed for the betterment of human civilization.

There are forms of power, however, which are subtle, defy measure and limit, and yet many times possess greater strength than physical sources. Think of the power of suggestion. How is it that the mere presence of tobacco, alcohol, or drugs to the addict presents such a temptation? Ideas planted as seeds in the minds of people can be very powerful and influential as well. Infamous twentieth century dictators such as Josef Stalin and Adolf Hitler began their reigns of terror by promoting ideas that attracted a following. The power of words, both aural and written, defies measure and limit. Martin Luther King, Jr. stirred the hearts of African-Americans when he proclaimed at the end of his famous "I Have a Dream" speech at the foot of the Lincoln Memorial during the August 1963 March on Washington, "Free at last, free at last, thank God Almighty, we are free at last!" Less than three years earlier, John F. Kennedy in his inaugural address had challenged the American people to act, stating, "Ask not what your country can do for you, ask what you can do for your country."

Power can be confined and measured or it may defy any quantifiable bounds, but power in all its forms moves us, in mind, soul, or physical body from one point in life to another. It is the operative power of God, which possesses no limits, can be seen, felt, and experienced, and at the same time can be so subtle that it does not appear to be present, that controls our world through creation, redemption, and sanctification. It is God's action in the world, the powerful and subtle, which, if understood and heeded, can bring our world greater wholeness and unity in imitation of the oneness of God.

God's power is omnipresent. The created world, visisble in the changing of the seasons, the daily weather patterns, and the dynamic nature of our earth, demonstrates how God's power is operative in our world. God's power in creation is readily visible in the beauty which surrounds us; it is a gift made for the enjoyment, care, and use of God's greatest creation, the human race. God's power and action was next seen in the redemptive life of Jesus Christ. In his life as teacher, miracle worker, and reconciler,

Jesus taught us how to live, to love, and to grow in God's grace and providence. God's power is also present in the work of sanctification brought by the Holy Spirit. It is the Spirit of God which acts each day bringing light to God's creation and renewal to the seed of faith planted at our baptism.

God's power is present all about us — it can be seen, felt, and experienced. God's creative, redemptive, and sanctifying action in the world eludes bounds and measurement; it is a free gift provided by our loving Father to his greatest creation. Yet, unlike all physical manifestations of power, both those in nature and those with human origins, God's power is not thrust upon us in a way that gives us no choice. As with all God's gifts, we have the opportunity to accept or reject God's power. We can abuse God's creation and destroy its potential for future generations. We need not be saved; we can ignore Jesus' teaching and example. God does not place us in a straightjacket and demand compliance, rather God always gives us a choice; the decision is ours to accept or reject God's grace. We must believe in the power of God in our lives and its strength to overcome evil. Our union with God and confidence in God's action are essential elements in the daily walk in faith. May we respond to God's power and action in the world. Let us live the faith given us by Jesus and guided by the Holy Spirit, proclaiming in our words and actions the power of God in our lives.

Application Of The Parable To Contemporary Life

Sermon Openings
1. "Four score and seven years ago, our fathers brought forth on this continent a new nation conceived in liberty and dedicated to the proposition that all men are created equal." These words of President Abraham Lincoln at the dedication of the Gettysburg National Cemetery will always be remembered by students of American history. The year was 1863; the nation was in the midst of the great Civil War. After 87 years of unity, the great house which was the union was divided. President Lincoln was familiar with the Bible. He must have read today's Gospel passage, for he knew that a house divided could not stand.

Abraham Lincoln looked for what was permanent in the life of the nation. He looked for that which would last forever. For Lincoln it was the principles of democracy which would live forever. That is why he finished his famous "Gettysburg Address" with the words, "that government of the people, by the people, for the people shall not perish from the earth!"

The Civil War, certainly the most written about and traumatic of disasters in American history, was a time when the unity of the country was compromised. Divided, the nation was not able to perform as it had in the past. Working separately, the Union and the Confederacy could only provide a facsimile of what the nation could be. In division each side missed part of the strength it formerly enjoyed.

The Civil War and the efforts of President Abraham Lincoln to heal the wounds of division illustrate Jesus' point in today's Gospel that any unity divided will ultimately fall. For each Christian there must be personal unity with Jesus. Without this union evil can find a foothold and destroy us. We are challenged in today's Scripture reading to maintain our union with Christ as the relationship necessary for eternal life.

2. Today people throughout the world refer to the Hawaiian islands as "paradise." Visitors come to enjoy the plush beaches, the warm weather, and the friendly atmosphere that has become a trademark of the islands. In the mid-nineteenth century, however, Hawaii, especially the island of Molokai, was not so inviting. The northwest section of this little island was home to victims of Hansen's Disease, commonly known as leprosy. People from throughout the world were ferried to this spot by ships that were more like prisons than vessels of transportation. Ship captains maneuvered close enough to shore so that the unlucky passengers had at least a chance to make it to land. Because lepers were believed to be highly contagious the ship did not dock. Passengers were thrown over the side. Those who could swim made it to shore; many others drowned.

A small settlement, Kalapapa, was started on the island by the lepers themselves. Their daily existence was one of true misery as they slowly, day by day and one by one, succumbed to the debilitating and disfiguring effects of their common affliction. The outside world cared little for the plight of these people. Molokai's isolated location was a perfect spot, it was thought, to keep these people away from society.

There was one man who cared, one person who was willing to demonstrate that God cared for all, not merely those without leprosy. Joseph de Veuster, a Belgian missionary priest who took the name Damien, came to Molokai in the early 1870s to minister to those who had been abandoned by society. Damien was not only the priest of the settlement, he was the doctor, the social worker, and possibly most important, the friend of all in the Kalapapa settlement. Daily Damien would attend to the needs of his brothers and sisters. He dressed their wounds, dried their tears, listened to their stories, and prayed with them and for them. Each Sunday in his sermon Damien began, "You the lepers of Kalapapa ..." His message spoke to the people of how the power of God was with them in their time of trial. God would always remain faithful for God could act in no other way.

One day, after many years of labor among the lepers of Molokai, Father Damien mounted the pulpit to address his people. His usual opening contained a subtle but very important difference. He began, "We the lepers of Kalapapa ..." Father Damien had become one with the people he served in every way. Damien died in April 1889, a victim of the very disease that had claimed so many to whom he ministered faithfully.

Father Damien was a minister of God who accepted people for who they were. He was not concerned that they were sick or had been judged by society as unworthy of care. He realized that all who seek God, listen to his voice, and do their best to carry out the Lord's commands are members of God's family. All can be brother and sister to the Lord. In today's Gospel we hear how Jesus excoriates those who make war against God, those who believe Jesus to be in league with Satan. Those who do the will of God, many of whom are the "lepers" of contemporary society, are the true brothers and sisters of the Lord.

Points Of Challenge And Questions To Ponder

1. Do we believe in the triumph of righteousness over evil, of the victory of Christ over Satan? Do we live our lives with hope in the final resurrection from the dead or has the world and its perversion of evil darkened our view?

2. Are we team players with Jesus? Do our efforts support or hinder his mission to build the Kingdom of God in our world? Are we team players in the world? Are we willing to work with others in order to benefit the whole? Are we people who would rather "go solo"? Can we trust others to be present or do we place hope and confidence only in ourselves?

3. Do we believe in the power of God in our lives? Can we perceive God's action in the world or do we allow ourselves to remain in the dark? Do we have the faith to see the victory of God over the forces of evil?

4. Do we concentrate on the negative in life? Do we see the glass of water as half empty and think about all that we cannot do? Can we, rather, look at the glass as half full and see all the things that we can do and have accomplished?

5. Do we make our best efforts to bring unity and harmony to the various situations in life? Do people see our actions as restorative and unifying or do they experience what we do as divisive? Do we rally people together or is our attitude one that alienates others?

Exegesis And Explanation Of The Parable

This passage sheds light on the meaning of Mark's Gospel as a whole. Ordinary, unlettered people, recognizing the goodness and God-given character of Jesus, flocked to him while those who might have been expected to share this attitude, his family and the religious leaders of the people, kept their distance. They not only failed to perceive the true source of Jesus' mission and the special character of his actions, but they went further and attributed them to evil sources. This pericope thus aids the evangelist in demonstrating to his readers the true identity of Jesus as Lord and Messiah. Mark builds his case for Jesus' divine position and authority throughout the first half of his Gospel, reaching its climax with Peter's confession in 8:29: "You are the Messiah."

Mark constructs this passage using the literary technique of framing in order to highlight certain pericopes as central to his message about Jesus. Verses 20 and 21 tell us that Jesus' family came to take charge of him, saying, "He has gone out of his mind." This scene continues in verse 31 when his family arrives and Christ presents his teaching on who his family truly is. Sandwiched or "framed" between the story of Jesus' family, three proverbs or short parables that illustrate the Lord's mastery of evil and Satan are presented by Mark. This technique is used to direct the reader to the importance of the central message of the identity of Jesus. In claiming power over Satan, Jesus demonstrates his divinity, for only God possesses such power. Mark uses framing elsewhere in his Gospel. The cure of the woman with a hemorrhage (5:25-34), inserted between the story of Jairus' daughter (5:21-24, 35-43), is the primary example.

The "frame" of Mark's first three parables is provided by the Lord's teaching on the nature and composition of the family of God. The evangelist opens this passage by introducing us to Jesus' family for the first time. It seems that word of Jesus' ministry in Galilee has reached them and they came to take charge of him, thinking him unstable. Mark returns to the family in verse 31 to expose the blindness of those who should have known him better, his mother, brothers, and sisters, and the Scribes who accuse him of being possessed by Beelzebul. Having described Jesus' appointment of the first apostles (1:14-20), Mark addresses the theme of the constitution of the wider family of the new Israel. Those who enter into a relationship with Jesus and are able to share with him in spontaneous obedience to the will of God are welcome. Those who respond are not the expected ones, the religious leaders of the day and Jesus' own family. These latter, in fact, disown him out of blind prejudice.

What the evangelist meant in referring to Jesus' "brothers" was a source of great consternation for many in the early Church. Patristic scholars produced three different opinions on the meaning of "brothers" used by Mark in verse 31. One view, the Helvidian (after Halvidius, circa 380), says that the word means blood brothers. Epiphanius, also writing in the late fourth century, believed the "brothers" to be the sons of Joseph from a former marriage. The Hieronymian theory, promoted by Saint Jerome, again in the late fourth century, stated that the brothers were first cousins, being sons of Mary, the wife of Clopas, and sister to Mary, the mother of Jesus. The first two views were popular throughout antiquity. The latter two are important, for they preserve the doctrinal view in Roman Catholicism of the perpetual virginity of Mary. Christians today, scholars and the general faithful alike, have not probed the doctrinal depth of the issue but see in verses 33 through 34 the more important and fundamental teaching that natural ties of kinship do not confer any special privilege or right of entry into the company of Jesus. Wherever Jesus is present he offers himself as a gift to all people irresepective of their background or descent.

Some contemporary scholars have questioned, however, the negative picture which Mark paints of Jesus' blood family, regardless of the passage's interpretation. Examination of the whole of Mark's Gospel reveals a similar attitude toward those in Nazareth who would have known Jesus and may have grown up with him. In 6:1-6 the evangelist excoriates those who wonder at Jesus' ability to preach and the wisdom with which he is endowed. The issue for Mark, one can conclude, is not to expose the unfaithfulness and/or misunderstanding of Jesus' family and friends but to demonstrate the danger of attachments to blood family, village, or tradition that are held above one's relationship with Christ. The evangelist thus is suggesting that people evaluate their priorities and order them as necessary to make Jesus and his message number one in their lives.

The heart or "framed" section of this important passage is centered about three short parables, the first preached by Jesus in Mark's

Gospel. Jesus used parables to reveal his message in a veiled way. Just as in his person Jesus did not preach from the housetops, neither does his teaching disclose everything openly to his listeners. This technique was used as a means of response to the spiritual blindness of his family and the religious leaders. These "parables" are more truly expanded proverbs used as a rhetorical device to turn the tables against Jesus' opponents, outsiders who have rejected what comes from God, by showing that any intelligent person would recognize the absurdity of the claim that Jesus is possessed by Beelzebul. The Scribes claim that Jesus' power to cast out demons was a sign that he had received his authority from the chief demon, Beelzebul.

The Lord's response presents in parable form two parallel situations — the divided kingdom and the divided house — that illustrate the absurdity of thinking that Satan can be at enmity with himself. Initially Mark wishes to demonstrate that the activity of Jesus was so remarkable that it can be associated with supernatural power; the only question is whether the source is God or Satan. Jesus accepts the power of Satan but turns it back upon the Scribes. The parable of Beelzebul teaches that the Scribes' accusation that associates Jesus with Satan is ridiculous. If Satan was responsible for the activity of Jesus he would be setting one of his subjects against the work of others. Clearly Satan would not be such a fool. If division existed in Satan's house there would clearly be signs of the demise of his kingdom. Since by the Scribes' own confession Satan's empire is not destroyed but still exists, then he cannot be at war with himself in his own domain. If good things are happening and demons are being cast out, another power must be at work. This passage is taken as sufficient refutation of the charge that Jesus' activities are Satanic in inspiration.

The second parable, verse 27, the story of the strong man, is designed to demonstrate Jesus' power and mastery over Satan. Some scholars suggest that based on pure logic alone Jesus' image of the divided house and kingdom is not convincing, suggesting that the parable of Beelzebul is designed to raise the question of whether Jesus is stronger than Satan. People believed Satan to be strong, but in this second parable Jesus is clearly the one who is robbing, as is evident in the exorcisms he has performed, releasing those who are vassals to the devil. The inference of the parable is clear — Satan has been "bound" by one stronger than himself. In the light of Isaiah 49:24 and 53:12, which speak of the strength of the Messiah, there can be no doubt that Mark is demonstrating that the power of the expected Messiah is present in Jesus. Mark also wishes to show that the exorcisms and other miracles of Jesus were an important part in illustrating the Messiah's great power over the forces of evil. People are challenged to recognize the hidden power of God at work in the ministry of Jesus.

The third parable, blasphemy against the Holy Spirit, has been a source of great discussion and much confusion over the centuries. The parable seems to be directed against those who should have been convinced by Jesus' actions that miraculous powers are at work, but who unequivocally say they are diabolical. Several different explanations have been made to understand Jesus' words. One interpretation says that all sins may be forgiven as long as people do not cut themselves off from the source of forgiveness, the Holy Spirit, who leads us to the Father and Son. Mark may also be referring to those who in his day have already cut themselves off from forgiveness, namely people who are persecuting the Christian community. Another interpretation says that those offenses that were pardonable before the resurrection cannot be pardoned in a time when the witness of the Holy Spirit is predominant. Still another understanding says that for Mark blasphemy against the Holy Spirit is the intentional failure of people to recognize the power of God and their need for his saving work. In essence such people were biting the hand that fed them, cutting themselves off from the possibility of salvation. Blasphemy against the Holy Spirit was an extreme form of opposition to God. A fourth interpretation links a sin against the Holy Spirit with the charge that Jesus is possessed by the devil. Exegetes suggest that there is no justification to expand the severe warning in verse 29 into a universal statement of the dire fate in store for those who challenge Jesus' claim to have inspiration from God. His opponents and accusers were the official guardians of religion who should have known God and God's Spirit already. Yet, even with this knowledge, they vehemently resist Jesus when he seeks to confront them. By declaring that Jesus' works are of the devil, they in effect set themselves up as judges of the work of God himself. This is the sin, the scholars say, that cannot be forgiven, inasmuch as the consummate position of the Scribes presents an impregnable barrier to the mercy of God.

Context Of The Parable

Context In The Church Year

These three parables of Beelzebul, the strong man, and the blasphemy of the Holy Spirit are presented to us by the church in the Pentecost period after the celebration of Easter. They serve as an introduction to the parables of Mark which will be presented next week. One of the central messages of Jesus is our need always to keep ourselves united to him. Earlier in this volume we discussed the Johannine passage of the vine and the branches, 15:1-8. Keeping close to Jesus, the source of our strength and life, requires constant reminders; we cannot rely on hearing the message only once. This passage, which associates Jesus with the divine and describes his mastery over evil, is sandwiched or framed within the context of how people viewed the Lord. Our view must always be that the Lord is central to our daily existence. The Church in its wisdom asks us to reflect on where we stand in our relationship with the Lord. This series of short proverb parables gives us this special opportunity.

Context With Other Gospels

The majority of Mark 3:20-35 is found in other Synoptic accounts, but not in the unified form found here. All three of the short parables are found in similar forms. Both Matthew (12:22-30) and Luke (11:14-23) describe the Scribes' accusation that Jesus is associated with Beelzebul. These accounts are more descriptive and contain additional information that most scholars think is attributable to the Q source. Matthew and Luke describe how Jesus offers a counteraccusation to that cast upon him by the Scribes: "If

I cast out demons by Beelzebul, by whom do your own exorcists cast them out?" (Matthew 12:27).

The parables of the strong man and blasphemy against the Holy Spirit are quite similar in all three accounts, demonstrating how Luke and Matthew are dependent upon Mark as a primary source. Some exegetes suggest, however, that Mark's source for this parable was different, but the preponderance of evidence does not support this theory. After the parable of the strong man, Luke alone adds the proverb, "Whoever is not with me is against me and whoever does not gather with me scatters."

Jesus' teaching on the family of God is also found in all three Synoptic Gospels. Matthew (12:46-50) follows Mark almost verbatim while Luke (8:19-21) omits Jesus' question but continues with the declarative statement common to all three, "My mother and my brothers are those who hear the word of God and do it" (Luke 8:21).

Context With First And Second Lessons

First Lesson: Genesis 3:8-15. This passage, drawn from the so-called second creation account, describes the first confrontation between God and Satan. Satan feels that he has been victorious through his seduction of Adam and Eve, but the author of Genesis shows that God is the ultimate victor. As Jesus demonstrates that he is stronger than Beelzebul in our Gospel passage, so God shows his mastery of Satan. The devil may have been able to trick God's greatest creation, the human race, but Satan must obey what God commands. Genesis, like the whole of Scripture, describes the ultimate triumph of good over evil, the victory of God over Satan. God as victor can rightly command obedience from all creation at all times.

Second Lesson: 2 Corinthians 4:13—5:1. Paul's words to the Corinthians serve as a great complement to the message of Jesus' triumph over evil. He suggests that we who walk in the footsteps of the Lord must keep our gaze fixed on what is eternal and not what is transitory. At times in our lives we may think that the forces of darkness have encompassed us so fully that there is no way out. Our faith and the words of Scripture, however, must convince us that despite the pain, hurdles, and gloom that exists in life, we will see in the end the victory of God. God has prepared a place in the heavens, not made by human hands, that will be our home forever. Our task while we walk this earth is to follow as best we are able in Jesus' path and to live by the message he gave us. If we can the victory of eternal life will be our reward.

Chapter 5

Awaiting The Kingdom Of God

Mark 4:26-34

He also said, "The kingdom of God is as if someone would scatter seed on the ground, and would sleep and rise night and day, and the seed would sprout and grow, he does not know how. The earth produces of itself, first the stalk, then the head, then the full grain in the head. But when the grain is ripe, at once he goes in with his sickle, because the harvest has come."

He also said, "With what can we compare the kingdom of God, or what parable will we use for it? It is like a mustard seed, which, when sown upon the ground, is the smallest of all the seeds on earth; yet when it is sown it grows up and becomes the greatest of all shrubs, and puts forth large branches, so that the birds of the air can make nests in its shade."

With many such parables he spoke the word to them, as they were able to hear it; he did not speak to them except in parables, but he explained everything in private to his disciples.

Theme

Life experience demonstrates that most things that are big and great did not start that way. Many great scientific discoveries began with a few mathematical equations on a chalkboard and a basic theory of operation. Numerous political movements started when a small group of people possessed a vision for the future.

69

Some of the greatest companies began as door-to-door sales or as a single shop in one location. Only with faith is it possible to have the trust and confidence necessary to see how things that seem so insignificant can with time become ideas, companies, or people that transform society. If we can trust God to do the work that is beyond us, then the difficult we can do today and the impossible we can tackle tomorrow.

Spiritual Food For The Journey

A group of botanists was exploring almost inaccessible regions in search of rare and new species of flowers. One day the chief of the expedition spied a rare and very beautiful flower located deep in a ravine that was guarded on both sides by tall and sheer cliffs. The only way to reach the flower was for someone to be lowered over the side on a rope. There was a young man who was observing the scientists at their work. The leader of the group came to the youth and said, "We will give you twenty dollars if you will go over the ledge on a rope and retrieve a rare flower for us." The young man looked the situation over and responded, "Wait one minute. I'll be right back." The youth ran off and returned a few minutes later accompanied by an older man. Approaching the botanist the young man said, "I'll go over the side and retrieve your flower as long as this man holds the rope. He is my father."

Who or what do you trust in life? Some people may answer that they trust members of their family, other relatives, and close friends. This would be a good and certainly an appropriate answer. When problems arise or obstacles are found along the road of life it is only natural to seek those who share our home and are integrally involved with our lives. Others may answer that they place their trust and confidence in things. In certain cases this too may be an appropriate response. If we find ourselves stranded somewhere, the fact that we have a VISA, Mastercard, or similar internationally accepted device that can obtain money, lodging, food, and transportation would certainly come in handy. Some people can only trust themselves. We have all heard and probably exercised the expression which says, if I want it done right I will do it myself. There are those in our world, however, who when asked the question, "Who or what do you trust?" could honestly answer, "I trust God."

Ultimately, as helpful as people and the material world can be, we must place our trust and confidence in God. God and God alone is the final answer to the pain, difficulty, misunderstanding, and loss that life can bring. We must do what we can do as best we are able and then we must allow God to act. Many people cannot place their confidence in God because the Lord is not visible; others fail to see the action of God before them and thus feel certain situations need the immediate "fix" that the visible world can bring. The parables of the growing seed and the mustard seed tell us that we must be like the farmer, who sows and then with patience and trust waits for the magnaminity of God to be manifest. God will act, and although it may at first seem insignificant, like a mustard seed, the kingdom that comes will be beyond our imagining.

Application Of The Parable To Contemporary Life

Sermon Openings
1. John Harding had it all; his credentials were impeccable. He had a wonderful family. His wife, Sally, was one of those people everyone enjoys meeting. His eight-year-old son, Rick, was a good student, enjoyed athletics, and obeyed his parents. John himself had moved up the corporate ladder. After graduating from Arizona State University, where he played baseball well enough to be offered a professional contract, he moved to California's "Silicon Valley" and signed on with one of the many software companies with headquarters in the region. Through his brains, diligence, and much hard work he rapidly moved into management, beginning at the bottom and moving up. Still in his thirties, national publications such as *Forbes, USA Today*, and *The Wall Street Journal* commented favorably on his managerial style. John Harding had the perfect resumé for life: academic achievement, awards, and many positions of importance.

With such a record it was not a big surprise when Millennium, the third largest software manufacturer in the world, offered Harding a special position; they asked him to be their chief executive officer. John jumped at the offer. Not only was it a great position, but it would allow him to return to his native New England. He settled in his home town of Boland, New Hampshire, only twenty miles or so from Concord, the world headquarters for Millennium.

Everything seemed to be going well for John. The town welcomed a favorite son; the company liked their new boss. Then in the twinkling of an eye everything changed for John Harding. Sally and Rick were riding in the family car. A drunk driver crossed the centerline and an instant later they were both gone. John Harding had the perfect resumé for life; he had no resumé for death. He was a man who placed all his trust in his own ability; he never had to rely on others. Now, however, in grief and shock, he crawled into a shell of mourning and refused to come out.

After a couple of months an old friend, Bill West, came to John to see if he could pull him from his state of grief. He knew that John liked baseball; maybe he would consider being the manager of one of Boland's four summer little league teams. Harding tried to run away, but Bill West was persistent and so John agreed. His team was the Angels.

It was at this time that John Harding met little Timmy Noble. Timmy, a member of the Angels, was eight years old and a towhead just like his son Rick. Unlike his son, however, Timmy was not a good player; he did not have the gifts for baseball. He did not possess the keen eye to be a good hitter and he did not have the strong arm needed to be a good fielder. But Timmy Noble had some very important qualities nonetheless. He had courage and a big heart — how can one measure such qualities? He had determination and, most especially, Timmy Noble had faith. He didn't worry about what he couldn't do; he was grateful for what he had. He had decided a long time ago to place his trust in God.

The Angels did well that year; in fact they won the league championship. Timmy Noble was not one of the stars; he just was not gifted as a baseball player. But there was something wrong, something radically wrong. Timmy Noble was very sick. He never told anyone; he never complained. He came to every practice and played in each game, even though he had to ride his bike five miles each way to the field. When the season was over and it was revealed that Timmy Noble had terminal cancer, John Harding knew the reason that God had led him to manage the Angels. John had the perfect resumé for life; Timmy Noble had the perfect resumé for eternal life.[1]

Are you a person who places all your trust in yourself or can you let go and allow God to operate in your life? Jesus in his parable of the growing seed suggests that we must do what we can do and then allow God to act in our lives.

2. Between 1955 and 1968 the Civil Rights movement transformed the United States of America. The beginning of this drive to human freedom did not start in a glorious and auspicious way; it was subtle and barely recognizable. Although Abraham Lincoln had signed the Emancipation Proclamation in 1863, freeing all slaves in the Confederate states; and the thirteenth, fourteenth, and fifteenth amendments to the Constitution, which guaranteed rights to all citizens regardless of color, were all in place by 1870, the experience of black America in 1955 was one of segregation and racism. On December 1, 1955, however, a seed was planted that would cause a revolution. Mrs. Rosa Parks, returning home from work on a Montgomery, Alabama city bus refused to move to the back of the vehicle when ordered to do so by the driver. "Jim Crow" segregation mandated that blacks sit or stand in the back of the bus only. Mrs. Parks was arrested and temporarily jailed, but word spread rapidly and she was released.

The incident was small, hardly worth mentioning in any usual situation, but these were special times in Montgomery. Martin Luther King, Jr., a young pastor at Dexter Avenue Baptist Church, was asked to lead the black community in a citywide boycott of the bus system. Led by Dr. King the boycott was almost total. Car pools and walking became the principal modes of transportation for almost the entire black community. It took just over a year, but finally in December 1956, the city buses of Montgomery were integrated.

Rosa Parks' courage and the rise to prominence and community leadership of Martin Luther King, Jr., initiated a series of events that eventually broke down the barriers of racism and ended the Jim Crow system of segregation which had been practiced in the South for nearly 100 years. From Montgomery the movement went to Greensboro, North Carolina, where four black college students demanded that they be served at a local all-white Woolworth's lunch counter. The Freedom Ride of 1961 was followed by other non-violent protests, including the voting rights march from Selma to Montgomery, Alabama in 1965. In August 1963 Dr. King closed the March of Washington with his famous "I Have A Dream" speech. Over the next five years the Civil Rights movement continued to grow, making inroads into the slums of Chicago as well as the urban areas of the South.

In April 1968 Dr. King came to Memphis, Tennessee, to support a sanitation workers' strike. He gave an electrifying speech to an assembled group where he exclaimed, "I have been to the mountaintop and I have seen the promised land." He had led his people through a dark valley that was beginning to produce light. The next day, Martin Luther King was assassinated; he was silenced at the tender age of 39.

The American Civil Rights movement began as one small voice saying "no," and it culminated with the transformation, legally and morally, of an entire nation. Few if any thought that Rosa Parks' refusal to move would result in a mass movement, but this is exactly what happened. It is like the mustard seed in today's Gospel that seemed so insignificant yet produced a bush so large.

Points Of Challenge And Questions To Ponder

1. Who or what holds our loyalty? When difficulty strikes where do we turn? Do we seek the easy and obvious answer or can we with faith and trust seek the ultimate solution which only God can give?

2. Are we people who seek control in our lives? Do we have a "need" to know that the situation is in hand? Do we only trust ourselves to handle the critical and difficult situations?

3. Is patience an important virtue in our lives? Can we step back far enough from a situation to relinquish some control and not fear that it "won't get done"? Do we possess the patience to allow God to operate in God's own time?

4. Do we allow the seed of new ideas and projects to germinate and grow? Can we see the possibility without the need to experience the final product immediately? Can we understand that greatness in anything cannot happen overnight?

5. What role do we wish God to fill in our lives? Do we wish God to be kept in reserve until such time as we need the divine presence? Can we perceive the presence of God around us in situations, events, and most especially people, or have we closed our minds to God?

Exegesis And Explanation Of The Parable

Chapter 4 of Mark's Gospel is one of only two places in the entire book (chapter 13 being the other) where the evangelist presents extensive teaching from Jesus. Commentators believe that the purpose of this instruction to the four apostles (Peter, Andrew, James, and John) was to implant the conviction that the suffering that lay ahead was to find explanation and denouement in the coming of the Son of Man, identified silently as the speaker — namely Jesus. The Lord teaches his apostles in chapter 4 that those who listen to him are assured that silent yet powerful forces are at work for them on the side of righteousness. This is as certain and unfailing as the work of nature, yet not all perceive the Lord's work (4:10-12).

Some exegetes have asked why Mark presents this collected material in chapter 4. One suggested answer is that the evangelist wants to provide some light to counter the gathering storm of controversy that is presented in the previous two chapters of the Gospel. Since Mark opened his book with the proclamation of the arrival of the Kingdom of God, it is necessary to express supreme confidence that Jesus can triumph over all opponents in due time.

The goal of the Kingdom is thus tacitly identified with the cause and work of Jesus and his followers.

The two parables presented in this passage, the growing seed (4:26-29) and the mustard seed (4:30-32), present a picture of the victory of God's kingdom. The evangelist wants his readers to know that although the present age may be frought with difficulties for those who believe in Jesus, and there may be little evidence of God's work, the seed that was planted by Christ during his time on earth will one day blossom greatly and become a mighty force in the world. Mark tells us that ultimately any opposition to Jesus will be ineffective. Trusting in God that the kingdom will come is strongly emphasized in the collective message of these two parables.

The parable of the growing seed (also called the parable of the husbandman) is difficult to understand because of its lack of context. Most scholars have pointed to the sequence — harvesting following sowing in due time — as the central image of the parable. It is highly unlikely that this was intended to refer to a gradual arrival of the Kingdom. Review of Jesus' teaching on the end times, and our knowledge of Jewish eschatological thought from which it was drawn, makes it extremely unlikely that he taught that God's reign would only come in a gradual fashion. Many commentators, in fact, believe that the stages of growth — blade, ear, and corn — are not part of the original parable. The length of the process is not emphasized, but rather the necessarily inevitable progression of growth. Spontaneity and the uncompelled nature of the seed's growth are the emphases. As a point of context, scholars point out that in 1 Clement 23:3-4 (written about 96 A.D.), a similarly worded parable is used to show how the Kingdom will not be long delayed.

Several interpretations of this parable exist in the scholarly literature. Some exegetes suggest the account is allegorical. Christ has sown; in time he will reap. During the interim the invisible work of the Holy Spirit in the Church and the human soul will continue. Protestant reformer John Calvin understood the ministers of the word to be the sowers of the seed. They should not become discouraged when immediate results from their efforts do not materialize. By reminding his followers of the process of nature, Jesus is telling the apostles that they must be patient to allow the seed to germinate and to grow. Calvin believed that Jesus' ministers should sow the seed and then go about the ordinary tasks of the day. As the wheat matured at the right time, so the fruit of the preacher's labors will eventually appear. Ministers of the gospel should take courage and continue their work, eagerly and faithfully. The Scripture scholar Joachim Jeremias suggests that God is the sower who allows nature to run its course, even to the point that it appears God has ignored the seed. However, when the hour arrives, God wields the sickle and this wondrous act initiates the Kingdom. The faithful are thus challenged to be patient and wait for God's action.

The preponderance of scholarship suggests that this parable is an answer by Mark to those who felt discouraged at the apparent lack of growth of the Christian community and the perceived failure of Christ's words to command the attention and respect of the world. Jesus' words indicate that life follows the normal order, like a seed which grows to maturity. The farmer is not anxious about the seed, for he knows the pattern of growth. The disciples should thus model themselves after the farmer and have faith in God to bring about the universal rule, as the farmer has faith in the process of natural growth. The parable sustains Mark's view that the dawn of the Kingdom, in its obscure beginnings, is hidden from human eyes in the ministry of Jesus. Nonetheless, Jesus' presence guarantees that the harvest of the Kingdom of God can be awaited with confidence. Mark thus challenges his readers to see that all who open themselves in faith to the future will certainly be freed from frustration and anxiety in the present age.

It is assumed that Mark aimed this parable of Jesus at those of his contemporaries who felt that by their own efforts they could hasten God's Kingdom. No special zeal for the law, revolutionary political activity, or preparation of the elect for the end will influence the arrival of the reign of God. Against all such ideas, Jesus teaches that the Kingdom of God will be brought about by God's power alone. Christ thus challenges his followers to build one's life entirely upon God's promise and no longer upon one's own ability or inability. When the hour has come and the eschatological term is completed, God will bring about the Kingdom; humans can only wait as does the farmer for the growth of the seed.

The parable of the mustard seed, verses 30-32, is another story of the Kingdom of God that presents a message related to the theme of the parable of the growing seed. There is little doubt that every Jew who heard Jesus' words could relate them to Israel's own experience. It was part of the social tradition that Israel had small beginnings, even inconspicuous. Indeed, the community had been destitute and enslaved at one time. Yet God never abandoned the people, but rather was ever present and has overseen the growth of the community into God's holy people. For the followers of Jesus the parable was equally meaningful. The unspectacular and outwardly insignificant ministry of Jesus may not look like the sort of thing that can usher in the Kingdom of God, but the parable of the mustard seed demonstrates that one cannot judge the significance of results by the size of beginnings. Mark applied the lesson to the evangelistic activities of the early Church as well as the ministry of Jesus. The insignificant beginnings of Christian missions must not daunt the missionary's faith.

Most recent commentators are agreed that the parables of the mustard seed and leaven (as included in Matthew and Luke) should be classified as "contrast parables." The central point of the parable of the mustard seed is the contrast between the insignificant and obscure beginnings of the Kingdom in, with, and around Jesus, and the magnificient ending that God has in store for those who are prepared to trust him in the quite unspectacular present. Mark's perspective on the parable involves a transference of situation. The time of the beginning, when Jesus sowed the seed or brought the good news, has now given way to the time of the Church's missionary promulgation of its message. In this latter time, despite hindrances and failures in mission, the Gentiles are being brought within the scope of the kingdom. Mark challenges his readers to perceive that despite the present insignificance of the day, the future is bright that God's purpose will be manifest in a triumphant manner.

Jesus' reference to the birds of the air nesting in the branches of the mustard plant has raised some questions in the minds of scholars. They suggest that Christians of the apostolic era would have interpreted the parable as a prophecy for the future growth of the Christian faith. Some commentators see the words allegorically as implying that the preaching of the gospel would bring all nations within the scope of the Kingdom. Old Testament references of birds seeking shelter under a tree (Ezekiel 17:23, 31:6, and Daniel 4:12) serve as the principal evidence to this interpretation. Other exegetes, however, use these same references to the Hebrew Scripture to suggest that verse 32 in its entirety was not part of the original passage, since none of Jesus' parables have references in them to Old Testament passages.

Verses 33 and 34 present a problem of inconsistency. Scholars suggest that verse 33 fits the original intent of parables, while verse 34 reflects Mark's understanding of them as designed to veil the truth from the outside. The latter verse emphasizes continual dependence on Jesus for the word. From Mark's standpoint this is an invitation to readers to recognize the deeper understanding of the word, but this is conditional upon their being drawn into the company of Jesus and their listening attentively to his living voice in the Church.

Context Of The Parable

Context In The Church Year

After the introduction to Mark's use of parable last week, we are today presented with one of the two major sections of Jesus' teaching in the whole of the Marcan corpus. The reality of our difficult world and the discouragement that at times comes with it necessitates that we focus on the victory won for us through the salvific death of Jesus. The parables of the growing seed and the mustard seed challenge us to see beyond the immediacy of our existence to the possibility that God can bring for those patient enough to await the Kingdom's arrival. The Christian community needs this periodic message of hope. We need to know that our efforts, which ofttimes seem so insignificant and worthless, will with time become not only important but so conspicuous that others, the birds of the air, will be attracted and seek shelter under our protection.

Context With Other Gospels

The parable of the growing seed (4:26-29) is unique to Mark's Gospel, although its message of trust, faith, and patience is found in many biblical passages. Matthew's parable of the wheat and tares (13:24-30) uses similar vocabulary to that used by Mark in this pericope.

The parable of the mustard seed is found in all three Synoptic evangelists and the Gospel of Thomas (20). Mark's version of the parable is is more precise than the other two writers, especially in its emphasis on the mustard seed being the smallest of all seeds. Luke and Matthew place this parable in tandem with that of leaven. The two form a pair which are two sides of the same coin. The parable of the mustard seed portrays the extensive growth of the Kingdom while the parable of the leaven describes the intensive growth of the Kingdom. Luke and Matthew also both say the mustard plant became a tree while Mark uses the word bush; the difference is not thought to be theologically significant. More importantly, all three versions of this parable teach us that although God's Kingdom may at first be inconspicuous, in the end it will be so conspicuous that those who are attracted to it, the birds of of the sky, can put it to their own use.

Context With First And Second Lessons

First Lesson: Ezekiel 17:22-24. The prophet Ezekiel wrote to the Hebrew people while they were in exile in Babylon. It is certainly understandable that the people may have lost confidence in God and felt they had been abandoned. Ezekiel reminds the people, however, that God will one day create a new Israel that will, like a majestic cedar that provides shelter for birds, be a place of refuge for the people. Those who have been made high and exalted will be lowered and those who have been humbled will be raised up.

Ezekiel's prophecy closely parallels the message of the parable of the mustard seed. God's kingdom has been planted, but it will take time for the mature plant to be seen. While the process unfolds people must trust in God to act. God's promise will be fulfilled; people need only be patient to witness its manifestation.

Second Lesson: 2 Corinthians 5:6-10 (11-13) 14-17. Saint Paul writes words of great encouragement to the Christian community at Corinth. He tells the people that if they can walk using their faith as a guide as opposed to their human vision, then they will possess the confidence necessary to wait for the presence of God in their lives. As we know, Paul expected the Parousia in his lifetime, but he realized that it might take some time. Patience, therefore, was a necessary virtue in order to experience the final revelation of Christ. We are all new creations in Christ; the old order has passed away and now all is new.

Paul probably did not want to wait for the coming of the Lord, but he came to understand that time was necessary for the Kingdom of God to grow in our world; it would not happen overnight. Maybe Paul had heard about Jesus' parables of the mustard seed and the growing seed and realized that he had to apply the teaching to his own ministry. We need to be patient for the Kingdom and allow God to act, with the surety that the wait will yield God's reign, which neither ear has heard nor eye seen.

----

1. Summary of: Og Mandino, *The Twelfth Angel* (New York: Fawcett Crest, 1993).

Chapter 6

Breaking Down The Barriers To Jesus

John 6:35, 41-51

Jesus said to them, "I am the bread of life. Whoever comes to me will never be hungry, and whoever believes in me will never be thirsty."

Then the Jews began to complain about him because he said, "I am the bread that came down from heaven." They were saying, "Is this not Jesus, the son of Joseph, whose father and mother we know? How can he now say, 'I have come down from heaven'?" Jesus answered them, "Do not complain among yourselves. No one can come to me unless drawn by the Father who sent me; and I will raise that person up on the last day. It is written in the prophets, 'And they shall all be taught by God.' Everyone who has heard and learned from the Father comes to me. Not that anyone has seen the Father except the one who is from God; he has seen the Father. Very truly, I tell you, whoever believes has eternal life. I am the bread of life. Your ancestors ate the manna in the wilderness, and they died. This is the bread that comes down from heaven, so that one may eat of it and not die. I am the living bread that came down from heaven. Whoever eats of this bread will live forever; and the bread that I will give for the life of the world is my flesh."

Theme

The path that leads to Jesus and eternal life is not an easy one. The vissicitudes, uncertainties, pitfalls, and problems in life can make our task of following the Lord quite difficult at times. Some of the barriers that come between ourselves and God are external and we have absolutely no control over them. There are many other obstacles placed in our path that are self-generated, consciously or unconsciously. We need to break down the hurdles, barriers, and obstacles that hinder us in our daily walk with the Lord and allow ourselves to be fed with the Bread of Life. Jesus will remove our weariness, lift our spirits, and bring us to life eternal.

Spiritual Food For The Journey

People who have served time in the armed services are quite familiar with an obstacle course. As a test of stamina, strength, perseverance, and courage, military recruits are often required to run a measured distance, many times through rough terrain, swamps, or hills, and successfully negotiate various obstacles, including rope ladders and cargo nets, high walls, tire mazes, and narrow elevated walkways. The course is intentionally made to challenge each person who runs it. Some people run obstacle courses with reckless abandon; they will do all that they can do to shave a few seconds off their time even if in the process they take great risk for personal injury. Others run the course with greater reserve; they are content to finish under the qualifying time.

Life is the greatest obstacle course and all people must run it, whether we wish to or not. Each day we are presented with various challenges, barriers, and hurdles that we need to negotiate to navigate safely to tomorrow. Generally we successfully conquer all our obstacles and move on to the next day. There are times, however, when the hurdles are too great, too numerous, or our earlier stamina is depleted. There are times as well through inattention, lack of forethought, laziness, and even sinfulness that we place

84

additional barriers in our way. Although life itself provides sufficient challenge, we compound the problem by our own action, inaction, or words.

Jesus' bread of life discourse provides us with contrasting images on the barriers of life and the way to navigate through troubled waters successfully. The Jews, those who heard Jesus' words after he fed the 5,000, had the perfect opportunity to remove some of the barriers that made life difficult. They had Jesus in their midst; the living bread from heaven was physically present and they failed to recognize him. In their ignorance the Jews placed a barrier between themselves and belief. Their inability to believe put God at a distance.

We are at times like the Jews; we place God at a distance and fail to feed ourselves on the Bread of Life. The obstacles of life are sufficient challenge for anyone, but they cannot be successfully conquered without the assistance of God. We need God and we need the nourishment which Jesus alone can give. We must feed on Jesus in the Eucharist, but we also must seek God's presence in Scripture and the Christian community. We place barriers before us. We ask, as did the Jews, "What is the bread of life?" We do not take sufficient time to feed ourselves on Scripture. Sometimes we are lazy; other times we claim we are too busy. There are those times as well when we simply refuse to listen. We often keep others at a distance. We will only associate with those who live in our same neighborhood, do the same work, or possess the same intellectual capacity. When we fail to see God in others, we miss a great opportunity and set up another barrier that keeps the Lord at bay.

Jesus, the bread of life, challenges us to break down barriers that impede our progress along the path to eternal life. We must seek the strength and sustenance which only Christ can give to assist us in removing hurdles and obstacles that keep God's grace at a distance. Christ's presence in the Eucharist, the Scriptures, and the Christian community feeds us with the spiritual sustenance we need in order to triumph over the obstacles, pitfalls, and painfulness of life. Alone we will be lost; with the Lord we will discover God's Kingdom, today and to eternal life.

Application Of The Parable To Contemporary Life

Sermon Openings

1. Jimmy Harper wearily plodded home after a tough day on the job. As he walked he spied a bench alongside the road; he stopped and rested. As he waited, a woman, hauling behind her a large cart of flowers, happened to pass by. The sweet smell of the flowers perfumed the air. Jimmy instantly lost the weariness in his body and his spirits were lifted. Never before had he experienced anything like this, especially from flowers, and he had many of them at his home. "How much are you asking for your flowers?" Jimmy asked the lady. "You may take as many as you wish," she replied. "There is no charge. Your gratitude and the proper use of the flowers is sufficient payment for me." Jimmy hurriedly gathered as many flowers as he could in his arms and, now renewed in body and spirit, continued his journey home.

When he arrived home and entered the front door, the sweet aroma of the flowers almost instantly permeated the house. Jimmy's wife and children came to the front room, sensing that something special was happening. They too had their weariness removed and their spirits lifted. The flowers were performing some magic; in a very real way these flowers were feeding the Harper family.

Jimmy was concerned that the magic of the flowers be maintained. When the blossoms began to wither and die, he gathered them together and planted them in a small plot of land behind the house. With sunlight and water the flowers again bloomed and continued their magic. Never before had the Harper family received such solace from weariness, comfort from sorrow, and spiritual nourishment as these special flowers brought.

Jimmy was quite cautious about the flowers; he did not want anything to happen to them. At first his caution was manifest only in a warning to his children, lest their energy in play result in trampling the flowers. Later, when the Harper children were more mature and guests were a regular occurrence at the house, Jimmy built a wall around the flowers to protect them. This caused much consternation in the family as now special permission was required and access was restricted to the flowers and to their special power.

Later Jimmy found it necessary to hire a guard to safeguard the flowers and lawyers and judges to adjudicate cases for access. In the process the family lost the special magic that the flowers had brought; they were no longer fed. In the end members of the Harper family, frustrated that the flowers were denied them, decided to seek the flower lady themselves. They searched the highways and byways; finally they found her. She was still giving away her flowers, free of charge, to any who would be grateful and would use them properly.[1]

Are you a person who lives to eat or one who eats to live? With respect to food, most of us, especially those who live in the so-called first world, would answer, we live to eat. Food is good and dining is pleasurable; it is a social norm. But for those who bear the name Christian, we must go one step further and ask this same question of our spiritual hunger. Do we live so as to be fed by that which God gives us, or do we merely eat and drink of God enough to survive? The story of Jimmy Harper and the flower lady challenges our motivation about how we think of God and remove barriers which impede our path to Jesus.

2. He came softly, unobserved, and yet, strange to say, everyone knew him. The time was the fifteenth century; the place was Seville in Spain. He came to announce peace and to proclaim the good news. He came to teach and to cure; he came to bring the light. As he walked by the cathedral, a funeral procession for a little seven-year-old girl was just beginning to form. He heard the sobs and pleas of the girl's mother. Moved with compassion, he asked the bearers of the funeral bier to halt. He touched the girl; she was raised to life once again.

The local cardinal archbishop heard about this event. Such displays of power were not to be tolerated. Such action led to faith which would only be dashed in the cruelty of the world. He was thus thrown into prison as a common criminal. In prison he was questioned by the chief or Grand Inquisitor of the city, "Why have you come? We don't need you here!" The prisoner made no response. The Inquisitor thus continued his harangue. He questioned the prisoner about his time in the desert, at the beginning of his ministry, when he was tempted with the great luxuries of power, wealth, and prestige. "You were a fool," said the Inquisitor. "You should have accepted Satan's offer! Why are you so bent on self-destruction? Why did you choose miracle, mystery, and authority over power, wealth, and prestige? There is no longer a need to believe in you and what you bring. Go away, you are not welcome here." This time the prisoner did answer, not with words, but with actions. He embraced the Inquisitor, kissed him, and walked out of the prison. He moved on to offer himself to another group at another time in history.

Fyodor Dostoyevsky's famous chapter "The Grand Inquisitor" in his equally famous book *The Brothers Karamazov* describes the rejection of Christ who has come to bring light, goodness, and peace to a world which needs him, but refuses to accept his presence. In a similar way the Bread of Life discourse in John's Gospel challenges us to open our hearts to the possibility of Christ and remove barriers that keep God at a distance.

Points Of Challenge And Questions To Ponder

1. When difficulties, obstacles, and the problems of life strike where do we go to find strength? Who is the source of life for us?

2. What barriers do we place between ourselves and God, whether consciously or unconsciously? Do we realize that these obstacles keep us from exercising our full potential?

3. Are we people who live to eat or eat to live in a spiritual sense? Do we rely on God to be fed or do we seek God only when we feel we need the Lord? Do we hunger for God or only "nibble" enough to survive?

4. Do we perceive the presence of God in our world? Where is God for us? Are we fed spiritually by God's presence in Scripture and the community of faith?

5. We spend a great deal of time in meals feeding our physical hunger. How much time have we spent lately seeking God and satisfying the spiritual hunger we experience?

Exegesis And Explanation Of The Parable

The sixth chapter of John's Gospel is a self-contained unity which shows evidence of careful composition by the evangelist. Its function within the Gospel is to portray the climax and turning point of Jesus' Galilean ministry. In this chapter we are introduced to Jesus as the bread of life, an idea which is systematically introduced through the sign of Christ's feeding of the 5,000 (vv. 1-15), followed by the Lord's address to the Jews the next day (vv. 26-59).

Scholars have shown that this chapter follows the homiletic pattern of Philo and Palestinian midrash. The model begins with a citation from Scripture and is followed by a detailed commentary on the passage. In this pericope, 6:3, "He gave them bread from heaven to eat," extracted from Exodus 16:4, is the the Scripture passage and verses 35-50 are the homily. Thus, commentators describe John 6:35-50 as a Jewish-Christian construction following the typical homily pattern of the day. Some exegetes have taken the homily idea of John chapter 6 one step further. It appears from 6:4 that the Feast of Passover was the setting for the whole of this instruction. Jewish synogogal readings for the Passover season, using the second of a three-year cycle of Scripture, featured Exodus, chapters 11-16. Since John's theme of the bread from heaven is related to Exodus 16 it is possible that the chapter is a medley of material drawn from Jewish religious practice of the season.

Jesus' claim, "I am the bread of life," is the first of the many "I am" sayings of John's Gospel. This is a distinctive case of Jesus' language of revelation in the fourth Gospel. There are seven different declarations of the Lord: (1) the bread of life (6:35, 41, 48); (2) the light of the world (8:12, 9:5); (3) the door (10:7, 9); (4) the good shepherd (10:11, 14); (5) resurrection and life (11:25); (6) the way, truth, and life (14:6); (7) the true vine (15:1, 5). All of these similitudes identify Jesus with symbols common to Near Eastern religious and human experience. Through the use of these common symbols Jesus declares that the people's religious needs and human longings are satisfied in him. They also provide an alternative to the more traditional titles used to identify Jesus, suggesting that no one title can contain the totality of Jesus' character.

The term "bread of life" is not found in the context of Jewish texts that describe manna. The oldest comparable text comes from the Babylonian Adapu myth in which the sky god Anu orders the food and drink of life to be served to Adapu. This demonstrates that the concept of a food which gives immortality is very old. The Jewish apocryphal work "Joseph and Aseneth" offers another parallel. In this book Joseph says that a God-fearing person (a Jew) eats "blessed bread of life" and drinks "blessed drink of immortality" and is anointed with the "blessed oil of imperishability." Later in the text the same promise is made to Aseneth. Later still, Aseneth eats a honeycomb given her by an angel who says, "See now you have eaten the bread of life and drunk the drink of immortality...." Scholars suggest that John's use of the expression "bread of life" most probably comes from this Jewish propaganda text.

John 6:35 is fundamental to the whole bread of life discourse. Jesus' self-revelation as the bread of life is expanded by the twin images of hunger and thirst that are filled with symbolic overtones. The verse is constructed as a synonymous parallel with the first expression, "whoever comes to me," interpreted by the second, "whoever believes in me." Coming to Jesus means believing in him. These twin images are more than rhetorical decoration; they represent a whole conceptual background. The Exodus 16 typology linked the gift of manna and water from the rock. Wisdom literature provides an additional perspective on this linking of food and drink. Proverbs 9:5 states, "Come, eat of my bread and drink of the wine I have mixed." In Sirach 24:21 we read, "Those who eat of me will hunger for more and those who drink of me will thirst for more." When we recall that Wisdom herself was sent from heaven in order to live among the sons of men, it is probable that John had these texts in mind when composing this section of his Gospel. A final example of this typology is found in Isaiah

49:10. "They shall not hunger or thirst ... for he who has pity on them will lead them, and by springs of water will guide them." In calling himself the bread from heaven Jesus claims to be the revealer of truth and divine teacher who came to nourish all people. Clearly, John is telling his readers that what people need for life is provided in Jesus.

Jesus' claim that those who believe in him as the bread of life will possess eternal life is a complete contrast to the Exodus 16 story where those who ate manna still died. Thus, the evangelist is demonstrating in chapter 6 that what Jesus has done in the miracle of feeding 5,000 is not simply feed people so that the hunger of a day is stilled, but he has shown himself to be the resurrection and the life. He has given life to those who feed on his words, who have seen him and believed that he will save them on the last day. This gift, however, does not come without price to the giver. Namely, as will be seen in the final section of the discourse (vv. 51-58), Jesus gives his flesh. Scholars thus conclude that the passage can only be fully understood in the light of the crucifixion.

After revealing himself as the bread of life Jesus encounters opposition from the Jews. Echoing again the imagery of the Exodus (Exodus 15:24, 16:2, 7, 12; Numbers 11:1, 14:2, 27; Psalm 105:24-25), the Jews grumble against Jesus. They resent Christ's claim to be the bread from heaven. Believing themselves to be fully equipped with adequate knowledge of the facts of the world, they assume that Jesus cannot be the means of revelation. They are correct in concluding that the divine cannot be revealed in that which is human, but they err in thinking that the divine can only be revealed in a superhuman way. They do not recognize the presence of the divine in Jesus. The Jews' murmuring demonstrates their inability to believe in the incarnation.

The opposition of the Jews also provides the opportunity for John to provide further discourse on faith and unbelief. The exhortation to believe is thrust into the foreground. Theologically the movement from faith as God's grace to faith as a demand on humanity is highly significant. In spite of his knowledge of the action of God's grace, Jesus in John's Gospel insists on humanity's responsibility in belief. God's call must be met by a response from

91

all men and women. In opposition to the unbelief voiced by the Jews, Jesus renews his appeal for faith. God initiates the universal process of drawing people to Jesus, but this must be answered by human action.

This passage closes (v. 51) by returning to Jesus' teaching on the gift of life he brings in himself. The manna eaten by the Israelites met their immediate needs for sustenance, but since the people died it did not satisfy ultimate human needs. Jesus, "the living bread come down from heaven," does not fulfill human need; those who eat the bread from heaven receive the gift of eternal life. The promise that one will live is analogous to the promise (v. 35) that any who come and believe in Jesus will never hunger or thirst again. God's will to give life to the world finds its ultimate meaning in Jesus' surrender and crucifixion, giving his flesh for the life of the world.

Context Of The Parable

Context In The Church Year

The need for Christ is ever present; it continues to grow with time and the complexity of life. Yet despite our need we often erect obstacles that make access to God more difficult. We need to be reminded periodically of our need for Jesus in the many manifest ways in which he is revealed to us. Jesus' bread of life discourse contrasts the Lord's promise of eternal life for those who come and believe against the barriers of unbelief which the Jews build. We must allow the Lord to operate in our lives and feed us with the spiritual gifts that assist us in our sometimes perilous journey through life. As the liturgical year continues the church provides this message of challenge and hope. The external barriers that life brings, plus those that we create, can be negotiated with the power of Jesus — our Savior and Lord.

Context With Other Gospels

The sixth chapter of John's Gospel is one of the many unique parts of this book when compared with the Synoptics. While Matthew, Mark, and Luke (as well as Saint Paul in 1 Corinthians 11:23-

26) all describe the institution of the Eucharist at the Last Supper, John uses the event (13:1-11) to emphasize the role of service in Christian life. John's Eucharistic theology is reserved for chapter 6, the bread of life discourse. As the earlier exegesis has shown, John uses this passage to give Jesus' self-revelation as the one who is needed for eternal life. Feeding on Jesus' body and blood will satisfy all spiritual hunger and thirst and provide the strength to continue the walk to union with God at the end of time.

Although there are no parallels between this passage and the Synoptics, there are several connections with other parts in Scripture. Exodus and Wisdom literature are used to provide the imagery of bread from heaven. John 6:35-50 also appears to be linked to Isaiah 55:10-11, where God's word fulfills its purpose as the rain and snow that come down from heaven fulfill their work.

Context With The First And Second Lessons
First Lesson: 1 Kings 19:4-8. Elijah was weary and afraid after fleeing from the grasp of Jezebel who sought his death. God was present to the prophet, however, and sent an angel to meet his need for food and drink. Elijah ate the hearth cake and water and was strenghtened sufficiently to do what was not humanly possible; he walked forty days and forty nights to God's mountain — Horeb. This story tells us that God will not only feed us today but will provide all that is needed for the tasks of the future, even if they are perceived to be beyond human capability. The story of Elijah is similar to Jesus' bread of life discourse in that the Lord's feeding allows us to do what is not humanly possible — attain eternal life. God will always provide; we need only to accept this free gift.

Second Lesson: Ephesians 4:25—5:2. Saint Paul tells the Ephesians that they are to strip away bitterness, passion, anger, harsh words, slander, and malice of every kind and replace them with the compassion and forgiveness which only Christ can give. We can only do this if we allow ourselves to be fed by Jesus through the Eucharist, the Scriptures, and the Christian community. The barriers of life which generate the vices Paul mentions can only be conquered with the aid of Jesus. Although in today's world many like to "go it alone" and others refuse to admit their need for anyone, the truth is that no one is able to navigate successfully through the often shoal-ridden waters of life without Jesus guiding the way. Fed by the Lord we will most assuredly find our way home to safe harbor and salvation.

---

1. Paraphrased from "The Flower Lady" in John Aurelio, *Colors! Stories of the Kingdom* (New York: Crossroad, 1993), pp. 146-147.

Chapter 7

Sharing With Others
In Imitation Of Christ

John 6:51-58

Jesus said, "I am the living bread that came down from heaven. Whoever eats of this bread will live forever; and the bread that I will give for the life of the world is my flesh."

The Jews then disputed among themselves, saying, "How can this man give us his flesh to eat?" So Jesus said to them, "Very truly, I tell you, unless you eat of the flesh of the Son of Man and drink his blood, you have no life in you. Those who eat my flesh and drink my blood have eternal life, and I will raise them up on the last day; for my flesh is true food and my blood is true drink. Those who eat my flesh and drink my blood abide in me, and I in them. Just as the living Father sent me, and I live because of the Father, so whoever eats me will live because of me. This is the bread that came down from heaven, not like that which your ancestors ate, and they died. But the one who eats this bread will live forever."

Theme

The world God created allows humankind to discover, grow, or manufacture anything we could possibly need or desire. God unselfishly provided the human race the abilities and skills needed to imagine and create almost anything. The Book of Genesis tells us we were all made in the image and likeness of God. The Lord did not have to create us or provide anything, especially the divine image inside us, but God nevertheless gave us all these things. God shared totally with the human race, including sending his son, the Redeemer. Jesus himself shared with us — his teaching and message, his body and blood in the Eucharist, and his salvific life and death. As God has shared with us, we are challenged to share with others. Jesus abides in those who nourish themselves on the sacred meal of his body and blood. We must abide with others by sharing all our hopes, dreams, and possessions. God has shared with us; we must share with God's people.

Spiritual Food For The Journey

We are all familiar with the adage, "It is better to give than to receive." We generally hear this around Christmastime or on other occasions when gifts are exchanged. Certainly everyone likes to receive, but the special feeling that comes from giving is one of the beautiful yet intangible blessings in life. We give because we want to assist others, bring joy, and demonstrate our love and affection. When we give to others we share something of ourselves — our resources, time, or expertise. For the gift to be accepted as a true indication of the giver's intention, it is necessary that the recipient feels that sharing is part of the process. A gift without sharing is a shallow gesture that brings confusion to giving and to personal relationships.

In today's world the virtue of sharing is not easily discovered. Today we are almost programmed to think of ourselves and do what is necessary to advance our own careers and positions. We spend a great deal of time (even years) preparing ourselves for the future. Certainly is is important to prepare ourselves, to exercise our talents, and maximize our opportunities. How much time, however, do we spend working for, sharing with, and being present to others? We spend a lot of time trying to meet our personal goals, but how much time and effort is spent meeting the goals of Christ — to be one with him, to share our lives with others, and to do our best to complete the work of building the Kingdom in our world?

God has provided all that we could possibly need or want, and it was given out of love. God shared with us in all things — providing for our needs and wants, endowing us with the intellect to help ourselves, and most especially sending the Son to redeem us and lead us home to salvation. We are challenged to share with others in response to God who first shared with us. Sharing our lives in all respects can at times be difficult, but it is always rewarding, providing us with many special blessings. Let us, therefore, not fail to be sharing people — who knows, as the author of the Letter to the Hebrews tells us, "By doing that some have entertained angels without knowing it" (13:2b).

Application Of The Parable To Contemporary Life

Sermon Openings
1. Sir Launfal, a knight-errant, methodically checked his list for the third time. He readied everything for his great adventure that would begin tomorrow. His sword was sharp, his shield was polished, and his horse was rested and fed. Finally he knelt down and prayed, "Dear Lord, tomorrow I begin my great quest in your name. Guide me in my search for your Holy Grail, the cup you used when you ate your last meal with your apostles. Make me pure, for only if I am pure will I find your cup."

He fell into a deep sleep and began to dream. In his dream it was the next day and he began his quest. He bid farewell to all at the castle and rode out the gates on his beautiful horse. Just on the other side of the gate, however, a beggar stopped him. "How annoying," thought Sir Launfal. At this high moment he did not want to be bothered by a beggar. Disdainfully, the knight flung a penny at the beggar and rode on.

Time, in fact many years, passed in his dream. He looked everywhere for the Holy Grail. He fought many battles but in the process he did not even obtain a glimmer of hope in his quest to find the Grail. Sir Launfal was discouraged. He had become an old man and had failed in his quest; he decided to return home. As he arrived at the castle gate the guard did not recognize him. "No beggars allowed here," the guard shouted as he drove Sir Launfal away. He was dejected; he felt alone. He had been rejected, even by those in his own home.

Finally the knight sat down and pulled the last crust of bread from his pocket. As he began to eat he noticed a beggar near him. It was the same beggar who had been at the gate so many years ago when he began his quest. Sir Launfal broke the bread in two and gave the beggar half. Then he went to a nearby stream and drew water for them to drink. As they ate and drank from his wooden bowl, Sir Launfal realized that the stale bread tasted as if it was fresh and the water was like fine wine. He turned toward the beggar, but he was gone. In his place was the shining presence of Christ. He heard Jesus say:

> Not what we give, but what we share
> For the gift without the giver is bare.
> Who gives himself with alms feeds three
> Himself, his hungry neighbor, and me.

The knight looked down at his wooden bowl. It was no longer there. Instead he held in his hand the Holy Grail. His search was now over.

At that moment Sir Launfal awoke from his dream. It was the next morning and he now knew what to do. There was no need to search for the Holy Grail; it was right in his midst. He only needed to open his eyes and share in order to find it. Sir Launfal came to realize his need for God present in the poor. By sharing his life he would find God. Today Jesus, the bread of life, asks us how much are we willing to share as the Lord has shared with us.

2. Once upon a time in a far-off land there lived a wise but old king. This king was very much beloved by his people, but, alas, he had no heir. Because he did not want his kingdom to fall into the wrong hands after his death, the king decided to choose his own successor before he died. Therefore, he promulgated a public decree that any person who thought himself qualified to be king should come to the capital city for an interview.

In a far-off village in that land, one young man heard about the decree and thought that he had the qualifications necessary to be king. He had good intelligence, was courageous, and he understood the government. Unfortunately, the young man did not have the resources of money, clothes, and food to make the trip to the capital city. His friends encouraged him, however, to set out. They told him that all he needed would be provided on the trip. Placing trust in his friends, he set out for the capital city to have his interview with the king. Along the way he was amazed to find that his friends were correct; all was provided for him. He was able to find lodging and a good hot meal each night in the village where he would stop. One family gave him a little money for those unexpected out-of-pocket expenses. Another family gave him a complete set of new clothes for his audience with the king.

After several days journey the young man reached a bridge which crossed over a mighty river which guarded the capital city on one side. As he was preparing to cross a tired-looking old beggar man came up to him. "Please," said the old man, "may I have the extra food that you have? I live in the forest where food is at times hard to find. And, if possible, can I have that nice jacket you have? It is quite cold in the forest, and as you can see I have nothing to wear." The young man thought to himself, "I have come all this way and now this old man asks something of me." After he had thought about it for a few more minutes, however, he decided that the old man needed the things more than he did. Thus, he gave the old man his food and changed clothes with him. Nevertheless, not to be deterred from his mission, the young man crossed the bridge and entered the capital city.

When he reached the palace he was told that the king was away and could not see him until tomorrow. Thus, the young man waited outside the palace all night for his opportunity to see the monarch. The next day, the young man was ushered into the palace by one of the guards. They passed down a long and beautiful hallway. The doors ahead of them opened. It was the king's throne room and he was holding court. When the young man looked up, he saw seated on the throne the same old man he had met on the bridge the previous day. The young man was confused and bewildered. "Why did you trick me?" asked the young man. "Why did you tell me you needed my food and clothes?" The king answered, "My son, I had heard from my royal officials that you were coming. You see, I do all of my interviews in the field. Although people think there are many qualifications for this job, there is only one that counts, the need to be one with your people by sharing your life. You, my son, have passed the test. You will be the next king!"

The young man discovered quite by accident that the qualifications for recognition by the king were much different than he expected. Christ, the King of the Universe, asks that we wake from our lethargy and assist others by sharing our lives in all that we do and say.

Points Of Challenge And Questions To Ponder

1. We spend a lot of time doing things that are geared to our personal advancement. How much time are we willing to spend in meeting the needs of others? How do we utilize the time we have been given by God?

2. God has given us all that we need and want. What have we given back to God? How generous are we with our time, talent, energy, and resources? Have we taken the opportunities given us by God to act in God's name?

3. When people call upon us for assistance, what has been our response? Have we made excuses or even lied so as to avoid our responsibilities toward others? What can people expect in our response to their needs?

4. Where do we receive the nourishment we need in order to do what we do? Is our sustenance found exclusively in the material world? What role or function does Jesus, the Bread of Life, serve in our lives?

5. Are we participants or onlookers in the work of God? Do we do our fair share to assist others, especially those who are most in

need? Can others count on us or do we expect them to conduct the business of building the Kingdom of God without us?

Exegesis And Explanation Of The Parable

The discourse of chapter six in John's Gospel, read over a period of five consecutive Sundays (Propers 12-16) in the Revised Common Lectionary, is understood by scholars to represent a collection of sermonic material drawn together under a Passover theme in much the same way Matthew drew together the material presented in the Sermon on the Mount (chapters 5-7). John the evangelist most probably used this chapter to transmit the tradition of the Lord's teaching at Passover time. After describing the feeding of the 5,000 (6:1-15), the Lord instructs his apostles and others on the meaning of this miracle. Then John presents two radically different teachings (6:35-50 and 6:51-58) that have been united as the bread of life discourse. The significant theological differences between these two passages have provided commentators much food for thought in their attempts to understand the evangelist's purpose and how we can apply this message from Scripture in our daily lives.

Historic interpretations of the bread of life discourse have been multiple. Patristic exegetes were not united in their understanding. The School of Alexandria, which tended toward an allegorical and scriptural exposition, understood verses 51-58 in much the same way as verses 35-50. Most of the Church Fathers, however, adopted a Eucharistic interpretation of this latter section. The Antiochene School, as well as John Chrysostom and Theodore of Mopsuestia, also stressed a Eucharistic interpretation. The Latin Church, seen clearly in the theology of Ambrose and Augustine, presupposed that verses 51-58 were a reference to the Eucharist. The bishops at the Council of Trent (1545-1563), however, were divided on the issue and made no decision on the question.

The latter half of the bread of life discourse presents several important teachings. When the Lord claims that the bread is his flesh he is bringing to its final unveiling the truth that he has been expounding since the outset of the discourse. Jesus speaks of himself as the bestower of real food for humanity (v. 27). He must not be likened to Moses in the story of manna, however, but rather to Yahweh. The insistence in verse 53 on both the fullness of the Incarnation and the participation in the Eucharist may be the evangelist's attempt to counter developing docetic or Gnostic tendencies within the Christian community which denied the bodily aspects of Christ. Jesus' teaching on Eucharistic gifts is divided into two sections. In verses 53-55 we are told that his flesh and blood are real food and drink that bring life. These special gifts bring about a lasting union between humanity and Jesus, the divine bearer of life (vv. 56-57). In verse 58 the evangelist brings together the whole of the discourse by stating that Jesus' flesh and blood is the living bread from heaven that gives indestructible life. John also shows how human participation in the life of Jesus is in actuality an extension of the interrelationship of Christ with the Father (v. 57). This passage also teaches that the crucifixion is the event that connects Jesus' claim to be the bread of life with the need to feed on his flesh and blood. In the Eucharist Jesus' salvific death is represented by his flesh and blood and applied in its redemptive force to all communicants. Thus, the celebration of the Eucharist also has the function of bearing witness to Jesus' incarnation and surrender to death. Finally, the figuative language of this passage is also instructive. John says that those who eat and drink of Christ abide in him and Christ in them. To be indwelt by Christ does not mean that one's personality is divided, but rather for the first time people will find true integration in their lives. This indwelling enables the believer to share in the divine unity itself.

This passage raises more questions than it solves in its teaching. Jesus' claim that people must eat his flesh and drink his blood leads to divison among his listeners. In raising the question "How can this man give us his flesh to eat?" the Jews demonstrate how many must have believed Jesus' claim to be pure error or nonsense. Others understood the claim to have true meaning in a spiritual sense. Jesus dealt with the dispute by being more explicit and more challenging in his teaching. Not only must people eat of his flesh, they must drink his blood. This statement, if taken literally, would have been highly objectionable to the Jews, who were forbidden to take blood. However, two points are relevant on this question. First, since John tells of no Jewish reply to this statement of Jesus, it may well be that the evangelist aimed these words, not toward the Jews who heard them, but toward Christian readers of the Gospel. Second, the twin terms of flesh and blood constitute a reference to the sacrificial giving and taking of life. Thus, in speaking of eating flesh and drinking blood, Jesus is saying that unless people come to live by his death and discover in their own lives the need for discipleship, they will never find the way to the life Jesus came to bestow.

The principal theological and exegetical question of John 6:51-58 is the apparent inconsistency between this passage and the rest of the bread of life discourse and the perceived change in theological understanding introduced here that is not found elsewhere in this Gospel. Verses 51-58 form a marked contrast to the previous course of Jesus' discussion and teaching. Some scholars suggest the evangelist is shifting his primary audience from the people in the story to the contemporary readers of John's day. Scholars almost universally agree that this section refers to the sacramental meal of the Eucharist, where flesh and blood are consumed, with the result that this food gives eternal life.[1] Those who participate in the meal can be assured of future resurrection. This teaching stands in opposition to John's thought in general and specifically to his eschatology. It also contradicts what he said earlier, for now the bread of life which the Father gives by sending the Son from heaven is the Son himself.

Various ideas have been postulated to explain the obvious differences in the metaphorical and Eucharistic sections of the bread of life discourse. One theory says that the evangelist could have written verses 51-58 intentionally as a continuation and application of the metaphorical section. Another idea says that John was aware of various audiences, namely unbelieving Jews and a group within the Christian community that held a false view of the sacraments. The different character of verses 35-50 and 51-58 could thus be explained by different audiences and intentions of the writer.

A third opinion says that the Eucharistic section was written by someone other than John, but from the same Johannine school. This represents a new stage of Johannine preaching that resulted from a rethinking of the bread of life discourse. A fourth theory says that the last section (verses 51-58) is an editorial addition which conflicts with the theology and purpose of the evangelist. This could be ecclesiastical editing that attempted to make John's Gospel, with its different theology, acceptable to the Church. Others suggest that this addition was necessary to defend the sacraments against the teachings of Gnostic groups present in the Christian community.

The question of the possible addition of verses 51-58 has been greatly debated among scholars and commentators. Rudolf Bultmann is the principal voice supporting the belief that this last section of the discourse was written by an ecclesiastical redactor to "correct" the chapter through the introduction of a non-Johannine sacramental theme that would make the whole discourse more acceptable to the Church at large. Many scholars believe this section to be added, but few believe the redactor's purpose was to "correct" the original text. Much evidence exists to support the claim that verses 51-58 is a later addition to the text. The main argument has been the contrast between this passage and verses 35-50, which contain a completely symbolic attitude toward the bread from heaven. More support is drawn from those who view the sacramental theology of verses 53-58, where the Eucharist is a material medium for heavenly and divine powers, in conflict with the evangelist's belief that only faith in the revealer sent by God is necessary for salvation. A third piece of evidence is found in 6:62-63. Here it appears that John is stating that flesh — Jesus' earthly state — is unimportant; all is dependent on the Spirit which is released by the ascent of the Son of Man, and manifested and communicated not in sacrament but in words.

Those who believe the passage to be an addition have also postulated its provenance. It seems clear the sacramental implications of this section would not have been understandable if preached to Jesus' contemporaries. Thus, many believe that verses 51-58 were taken from the Johannine narrative of the institution of the Eucharist, located in the Last Supper scene. This hypothesis accounts for a few facts: (1) the absence of the account of the Eucharist in chapter 13, (2) the close similarity of verse 51 to Luke's institution formula,[2] and (3) the clear reference to the Eucharist in verses 51-58 would have been understandable at the Last Supper.

While the preponderance of scholarly work supports the theory that verses 51-58 are an addition to the original text of John, arguments against this belief are present. Exegetes point out that the thesis of those who believe the pericope to be an ecclesiastical redaction is based upon the assumption that John would not have been interested in a sacramental doctrine. The doctrine presented in verses 51-58, however, is closely connected and (in the opinion of supporters) follows from the metaphorical concept of the bread from heaven. Some scholars comment that 51-58 does not at all interrupt the development of the ideas in the bread of life discourse, but rather raises the whole passage to a new, higher level of understanding. Second, some exegetes believe the whole discourse was planned to be Eucharistic from the outset. Lastly, scholars point out that an overall view of Johannine theology is not anti-sacramental or even uninterested in the sacraments, as many commentators have claimed.

Scripture scholar Raymond Brown, S.S. has suggested a compromise in the apparent conflict between verses 35-50 and 51-58. He believes that both pericopes present authentic Johannine tradition, but stem from different periods in the life of the Christian community. Brown maintains that the two versions of the bread of life discourse complement each other along the lines of word and sacrament in the liturgies celebrated by the majority of Christian denominations.

Brown's comment demonstrates how in the contemporary Christian community the two forms of the the bread of life discourse are understood. They represent a juxtaposition of Jesus' twofold presence to believers in the preached word and the sacrament of the Eucharist. This twofold presence is the structural skeleton of the Eastern Divine Liturgy, the Roman Catholic Mass, and those Protestant liturgical services that have historically evolved from modifications of the Roman Mass.

Context Of The Parable

Context In The Church Year
Each January the Christian community in the United States celebrates the "Week of Prayer for Christian Unity." This is the one time when all Christians are asked in a special way to concentrate on what unites and not what divides the Body of Christ. Ecumenical services are held in our churches and all Christians are asked to come together in a spirit of unity with the idea that ultimately we all have the same goal and ministry, although its manifestations and specific teachings do vary.

The ecumenical spirit generated in the Week of Prayer for Christian Unity can be ours year-round if we concentrate on the basics and find our strength and sustenance in Jesus, the bread of life. While our understandings of the Eucharist vary greatly in our churches, all Christians in some way celebrate and remember Jesus' last meal with his apostles. For Catholics this remembrance is central to their worship, but all of the Body of Christ places special emphasis on this ritual in its various liturgical services. In presenting John's teaching on the Eucharist, the church provides us with an opportunity to concentrate on what is basic to all Christian belief — the life, message, and hope of Jesus. Understanding our absolute need and dependance upon Christ is a message that must be proclaimed in our churches each and every time we gather in prayer.

Context With Other Gospels
The language about flesh in 6:51 and its development throughout this passage has made this one of the most controversial sections of John's Gospel. Since John, unlike the Synoptic writers, does not present a formal Eucharistic institution narrative, the theology of 6:51-58 has been the source of our knowledge of John's undertstanding of the sacrament of Christ's body and blood. John's Gospel complements the Synoptic writers in its vastly different

106

presentation of Eucharistic theology. Matthew, Mark, and Luke present the events of the Last Supper, Jesus' words of institution, and his exhortation to continue this celebration in remembrance of him. John's bread of life discourse gives the theological underpinnings to this special gift from the Lord. It also makes clear the connection between what Jesus gives in the Eucharist and his salvific death for all humankind.

Context With First And Second Lessons
First Lesson: Proverbs 9:1-6. This passage from Proverbs clearly demonstrates that God has been feeding us and sharing his life from the beginning. The Wisdom of God, present from the beginning, has built a house and spread a special table. Those who are simple and lack understanding — the lowly or *anawim* of society — have been invited to eat and drink at this special meal. God is ever present, but maybe especially to those who have special needs. We must forsake foolishness, advance in understanding, and come to the table of God. What is provided is absolutely free; our openness to God and his message is all that is required. God shares with us; we in turn must share with one another.

Second Lesson: Ephesians 5:15-20. Saint Paul writes of the need to make the most of every opportunity. Generally we are attentive in contemporary society to opportunities that will assist us in progressing along the road to personal success. We spend a lot of time preparing now for a future that is uncertain but one that we hope will be successful. So often, however, we intentionally or unintentionally miss wonderful opportunities today to share, with God and with one another. Since we are bombarded with suggestions of our need to move ahead and progress along the path of the world, we often feel there is no time for the things of God. Paul's suggestion that the Ephesians must be filled with the Holy Spirit, however, tells us that the things of God must be our highest priority. Let us, therefore, take every opportunity to be one with God and God's people, sharing our lives in all that we do and say.

1. The interpretation of verses 51-58 as a reference to the Eucharist is justified in two ways: (1) Emphasis on eating, feeding on, Jesus' flesh and drinking his blood. These words cannot possibly be a metaphor for his revelation. Eating someone's flesh was a biblical metaphor for hostile action, even the work of Satan. Drinking blood was a horrendous action forbidden by God. Thus, the only way verse 53 can make sense is as a reference to the Eucharist. (2) Since John does not have the words of institution of the Eucharist in his Gospel, verse 51, "The bread I shall give is my flesh for the life of the world" may be the evangelist's institution narrative. It resembles the Lukan form of the institution narratives. The main difference is that John speaks of flesh and the Synoptics of the body. Scholars point out, however, that Jesus probably used the Aramaic word for flesh in his speech since no such word for body exists in either Hebrew or Aramaic.

2. Scholars point out as well that the whole of verses 51-58 echoes Saint Paul in 1 Corinthians 11:24-26.